SHARKS OF HAWAI'I
THEIR BIOLOGY AND CULTURAL SIGNIFICANCE

SHARKS OF HAWAI'I
THEIR BIOLOGY AND CULTURAL SIGNIFICANCE

Leighton Taylor

Paintings by
Michael Cole
Comprehensive Register of Shark Attacks by
George H. Balazs

University of Hawaii Press
Honolulu

Cover Picture: *Galeocerdo cuvier (tiger shark)*
Tigers have a reputation as scavengers but their natural diet includes a wide range of living creatures: green sea turtles, monk seals, juvenile albatrosses, reef fishes, fishes, porpoises, octopuses, squids, lobsters, crabs and other sharks.

The scene in Michael Cole's painting is based on my observations of tiger sharks feeding on lobsters in the northwestern Hawaiian Islands and on the frequent occurrence of lobster carapaces in tiger shark stomach contents. The blunt flattened snout may be an adaptation for feeding in crevices and overhung caves. Divers collecting lobsters from reefs need to be especially careful.

Cover Insert Picture: *This fist weapon was collected on the expeditions of Captain James Cook. The teeth are probably from a gray reef shark.*

Page ii: *Megachasma pelagios (megamouth shark)*
This view of a megamouth shark suggests a way it may use its huge mouth to take in animals of the deep scattering layer (DSL) community. Michael Cole has painted a muted glow to the inner surface of the mouth. Perhaps this silvery covering reflects the dim light available and attracts prey animals. It is speculated that the lining of the mouth might have bioluminescent organs, but so far this has not been proven. Like Megamouth I, the shark in the painting has scars from encounters with a cookiecutter shark. The black spots on the lower jaws and chest and the black leading edges of the pectoral fins are characteristic of megamouths.

Page vi: *Carcharhinus melanopterus (blacktip reef shark)*
Blacktip reef sharks are common in the shallow, sandy lagoons of Pacific islands and atolls. Adults are found outside the lagoon along the coral reef drop-offs, but pregnant females enter shallow water to pup. The foot-long juveniles can be caught by hand in shallow lagoons by nimble waders. In the high islands of Hawai'i, blacktip reef sharks are now relatively rare compared with their former abundance. They can be seen reliably in springtime on the reefs east of Lāna'i; the area off Kawaihae, Hawai'i; the sandbars of Kāne'ohe Bay, the south shore and west end of Moloka'i; and near Olowalu, Maui. Juveniles have been reported to attack humans by biting them on the ankles or shins (see Randall and Helfman, 1973).

Published in North America by
University of Hawaii Press
2840 Kolowalu Street
Honolulu, Hawaii 96822

Printed in Singapore

Simultaneously published in Singapore by
© 1993 Times Editions
An imprint of Times International Pte Ltd
Times Centre, 1 New Industrial Road
Singapore 1953

Library of Congress Cataloging-in-Publication Data

Taylor, L. R. (Leighton R.)
    Sharks of Hawai'i: their biology and cultural significance / Leighton Taylor.
    p.   cm.
    Includes bibliographical references (p. 126) and index.
    ISBN 0-8248-1562-9: $ 19.95
    1. Sharks--Hawaii.   2. Sharks--Hawaii--Folklore   3. Folklore--Hawaii.
    4. Hawaiians--Folklore. II. Title.

    QL638.8.T38   1993
    597'.31'09969--dc20   93-10424
                                           CIP

Unless otherwise noted, all photographs are by the author.

Contents

Acknowledgments

Special appreciation is extended to colleagues who reviewed the manuscript: Bruce Carlson, Waikiki Aquarium, University of Hawaii; John McCosker, Steinhart Aquarium, California Academy of Sciences; Kim Holland, Hawaii Institute of Marine Biology; George Balazs, National Marine Fisheries Service, Honolulu; and Isabella Abbott, Department of Botany, University of Hawaii.

Thanks to the following: Linda Taylor for manuscript production; Michael Cole for color paintings; Maren van Duyne for line drawings of sharks, and Maria Taylor for their organization; George Balazs for contributing the important information on shark attacks in Hawai'i; and the many colleagues who provided advice, support, comment, and help with illustrations (including but certainly not limited to): John E. Randall, Arnold Suzimoto, Department of Ichthyology, Bernice Pauahi Bishop Museum; Tom Kelly, Waikiki Aquarium; Al Giddings, Kim Dodd, Rosa Chastney, Terry Thompson, and Margaret Hall, Images Unlimited; Foster Bam, Bam Productions; Howard Hall; Norbert Wu; Mark Dell 'Aquila; Marty Snyderman; and Tom Haight. Both the author and the artist extend thanks to Richard Ellis, whose masterful paintings in his 1975 *Book of Sharks* showed the power and utility of basing illustrations on the scientific record and informed imagination.

For research support (some recently; some over the past 20 years), I am grateful to the late Albert Tester, and to Robert S. Kiwala, Richard Rosenblatt, Carl L. Hobbs, Robert S. Jones, John Maciolek, Vic Faughnan, Rhet Mc Nair, James Parrish, Mark De Crosta, Marilyn Lowrie, Gary Naftel, Michael Palmgren, Richard Grigg, Edward Shallenberger, Steve Kaiser, Tim Tricas, John McCosker, Jim Luckey, Tad Luckey, Billy Al Bengston, James Corcoran, Roland S. Nolan, Richard Ellis, and Lester Gunther, Jr.; Robert Eichstaedt; Sayre Van Young; Bruce Carlson, Daryl Imose, Carol Hopper, Tom Kelly, Les Matsuura, Sara Peck, Marty Wisner, all of the Waikiki Aquarium; and Betty Kam and Patty Belcher of the Bishop Museum Library and Archives.

Although I never had the pleasure of meeting her, I want to express my profound appreciation for the scholarship of Mary Kawena Pukui in helping to document and interpret Hawaiian culture.

Introduction

Do you ever think about sharks? What kind of feelings does the image of a shark evoke in your mind? Is it awe, fear, respect, anger, admiration? All of the above? Chances are that the more you know about sharks and the more time you spend in and around the ocean, the more complex your feelings. Anyone in Hawai'i who dives, surfs, or fishes probably shares a similar complex set of emotions about sharks. But if your life and the survival of your people depended on the sea, your attitudes toward sharks might be even deeper and more complicated.

Some scholars have suggested that, in many ways, the ancient Hawaiians' sensitivity and knowledge of the sea far exceeded ours. As members of a culture long associated with the ocean, the ancient Hawaiians shared a vast lore and oral tradition about sea creatures. Sadly, only fragments of their knowledge have been passed on.

Undoubtedly they knew and believed much about sharks. Some of this ancient information is tangible and sharp-edged. The teeth of long-dead sharks (that might have swum beneath Kamehameha's war canoes) survive in the implements of ancient Hawai'i. Museums and fortunate private collectors guard the few tools, weapons, and artistic and religious artifacts that escaped loss. Although Honolulu's Bishop Museum is blessed with many such artifacts, important collections are also held in British institutions. I have had the privilege of examining many of them and comparing those ancient teeth with study sets I have assembled from sharks caught in Hawai'i.

Far less tangible are the words of long-dead *kahuna* whose knowledge of the sea has been incompletely passed to us by elders with a great respect for tradition but with reliance on often fragmentary sources. However, we can learn much from oral tradition, legends, customs, and the recounting of events. The attitudes of contemporary Hawaiians also give insight into traditional beliefs about the life of the sea.

What do these diverse sources tell us about the old attitudes of Hawaiians toward sharks? And how do they influence our opinions and experience?

My own interest in sharks has been

Isistius brasiliensis (cookiecutter shark)
Many biologists would love to see this scene in nature. No human has ever seen a cookiecutter shark take a bite from a tuna or other large fish. How does it get close enough to a fast-swimming fish like a tuna to take a bite? Perhaps it attracts them by the green, ghostly light glowing from the photophores on its belly. Certainly its large eyes help to find its prey. Perhaps the cookiecutter ambushes these fast-moving fish.

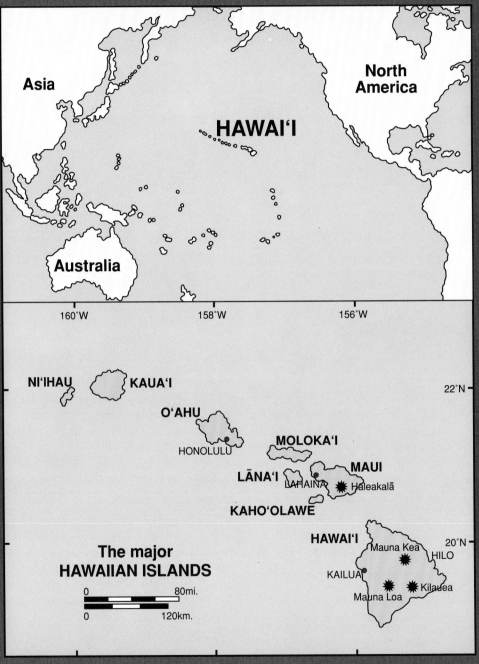

Asia

North
America

HAWAI'I

Australia

160°W   158°W   156°W

NI'IHAU   KAUA'I   22°N

O'AHU
                                    MOLOKA'I
          HONOLULU
                              LĀNA'I   MAUI
                                    LAHAINA   ✸ Haleakalā

                    KAHO'OLAWE

                                    HAWAI'I   20°N
The major   Mauna Kea   HILO
HAWAIIAN ISLANDS   ✸
                                    KAILUA
          0   80mi.   ✸   ✸ Kilauea
                                    Mauna Loa
          0   120km.

both personal and professional. As a sometime entrant in local long distance swims like the Waikīkī Roughwater and the Maui Channel relay, I'd like to know as much as possible about local shark biology. But as a marine biologist, with a love for Hawai'i, I yearn to know what the ancient Islanders knew, believed, and felt about the diversity of sharks in our waters. One way to learn, or to guess, what they knew is to interpret their artifacts and legends in the light of what we know today about shark biology and behavior.

Sharks are a diverse group. Worldwide, in shallow and deep seas, salt and fresh water, there are at least 350 species. Relatively few have been reported from Hawai'i. From the teeth used in ancient weapons and tools, we know the Hawaiians encountered most of the common species. We have no evidence (for or against) whether they knew such deep-sea forms as dogfish sharks or the 14-foot (427 cm) long megamouth

Although the whitetip reef sharks are often found resting in caves and reef crevices, they frequently make daytime forays over the open reef. Large groups like this are unusual.

shark, which feeds on deep-water plankton, that was discovered in Hawai'i in 1976. They must have known well the largest shark in the world, the whale shark; often exceeding 30 feet (914 cm), these calm plankton feeders still frequent our offshore waters. Their tiny teeth had little use and no artifacts using them have been found.

Because each species has distinctively shaped teeth, we can identify the kinds of sharks that Hawaiians used in their tools and weapons. We can only guess the species mentioned in oral tradition and passed along by such recorders as Kamakau, Malo, and others. We need to re-examine some of the guesses made over the years based on our contemporary knowledge of modern sharks.

Our modern knowledge of the biology of Hawaiian sharks comes from a variety of sources—including research at the University of Hawaii and other universities. The species found in Hawai'i are widely distributed in the warm waters of the Pacific and adjoining seas, and some forms are found in warm areas of the Atlantic.

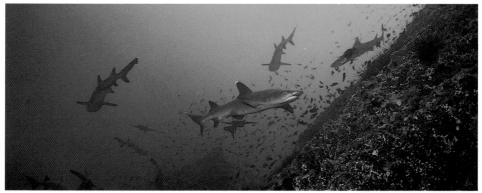

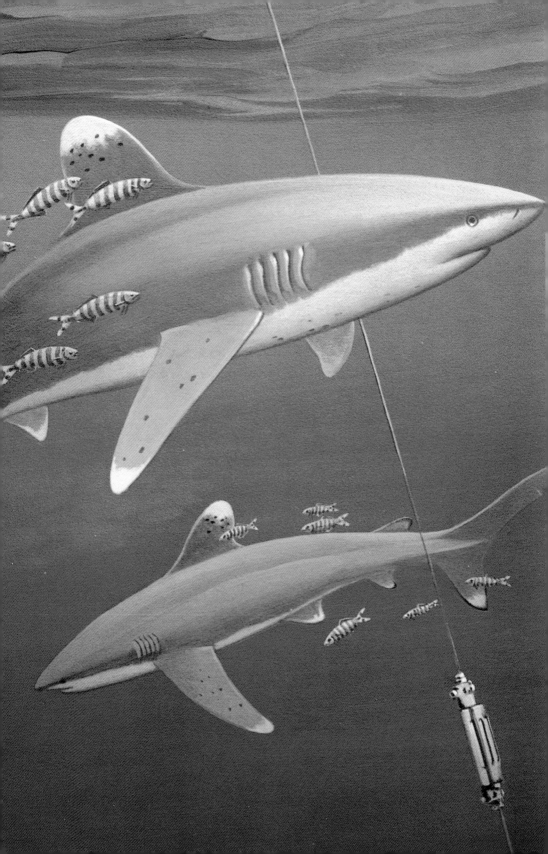

Basic Shark Biology

Definition of a Shark

A shark is a special kind of fish. Fishes are animals with vertebral columns and median fins that breathe using gills. Such a definition of a fish covers a wide range from tunas to stingrays. It includes the survivors of the ancient lineage of jawless fishes—lampreys and hagfishes.

In general terms biologists divide jawed fishes into two major groups based on a variety of characters but summarized in their common catchall names, bony fishes and cartilaginous fishes (or sharks and rays). These major groupings are based on the basic difference in the internal skeletons of bony fishes and sharks and rays.

There are numerous misconceptions about sharks. One of the most common is that sharks are basically all the same. As we learn more about these interesting animals, this generalization is dying out. However, it is common in writings about sharks to read such statements as: "the shark is a swimming

Carcharhinus longimanus (oceanic whitetip shark)
Carcharhinus longimanus *is well named. Its scientific specific name means 'long-handed' referring to the very elongate pectoral fins, tipped with white like the dorsal fin. When research vessels stop in open tropical seas to gather data about current patterns, they lower instruments on long cables (lower right). Curious oceanic whitetips often gather around the cables and research vessels, hence their other name, "oceanographer's shark."*

nose," "the shark is a living fossil," "sharks are color blind," "sharks have a rigid upper jaw and must turn on their backs to bite," "sharks have very simple brains."

It is a mistake to imply that every shark is the same as every other. There are relatively few species of sharks, about 350 species compared with more than 24,000 kinds of bony fishes, but within this relatively small group there is significant diversity—in size, habitat, behavior, and morphology.

Biologists seldom state an exact number of species of a group of animals. They usually give an approximation rather than offer a specific number. There are several reasons for this. Most biologists operate with the implicit faith that there are undiscovered species in the world. This faith has been substantiated by the discovery of such new species as megamouth (which also represents a new family), and there have been other new species of sharks discovered fairly regularly over the last half century.

As research on sharks continues, biologists sometimes find that two or more species names really refer to only one kind of shark. In a case like that, the scientific name that has been applied the longest is used and the younger name is set aside. Sometimes biologists find that a single shark name has been applied to two or more different kinds of sharks and new names must be given to the additionally re-

5

cognized species. Noted shark scholar Leonard Compagno reported that the family Carcharhinidae (ground, or requiem, sharks) is comprised of 49 valid species, but has had over 150 incorrect names included within the family.

Of course there are some characteristics shared by all sharks, but most generalizations about the group need qualification. Consider the myths at the beginning of this section. "The shark is a swimming nose" implies that all sharks rely principally on their sense of smell. It is true that all sharks studied have well-developed olfactory organs in their paired nostrils, the size and location of which vary with the species. However, sharks use a variety of sensory systems to find prey and to survive in their world.

Most sharks have a well-developed sense of vision. Sharks that are active in low-light environments (such as the deep sea or the nighttime reef) have a special structure in the eye called a *tapetum*. This reflective layer beneath the retina reflects light back to receptors, thus boosting the low signal. Some species, such as the great white shark, have been shown to have color vision.

Like bony fishes, sharks are sensitive to vibration through their lateral line organs. In addition, the ampullae of Lorenzini (jelly-filled pores containing nerve endings on the snout and head of all sharks) are sensitive to electrical currents given off by contracting muscles of all living prey—from shrimps to seals.

The statement that sharks are living fossils implies that all species are of ancient lineage. Although it is true that there are 400 million years of fossil record through which shark lineages

---

Sharks are well known for their sense of smell but they have excellent visual systems as well. Behind the retina is a reflective layer called the tapetum that magnifies the light signal for night-active sharks and sharks that live in the deep sea.

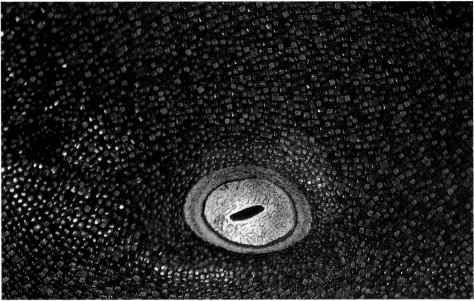

PHOTO BY TOM KELLY

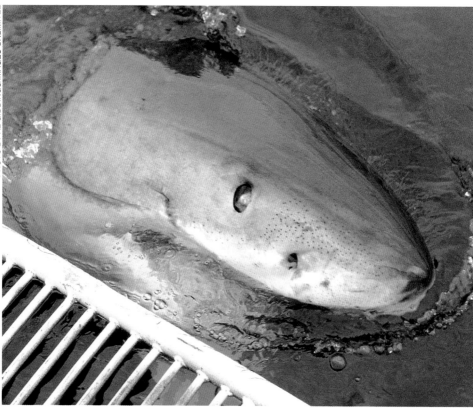

Above: *This great white shark is approaching the steel swim step of a fishing boat and preparing to take a bite of what it senses as prey. Note that the eye has rolled back into the socket to protect it from the struggles of a struggling prey animal (like a seal with long claws). Note the large nostrils. The many pores on the snout are ampullae of Lorenzini. They are sensitive to the electrical signals given off by metal in water as well as by tensing muscles of prey.*

Left: *There is a rich record of shark fossils extending for millions of years. Although sharks have relatively soft skeletons, they have sufficient mineralization to form fossils. This 160-million-year-old fossil from the lithographic limestone shows the vertebral column, dorsal fin, and spine of a horn shark. It looks very similar to the fins of the members of the family found in the world's temperate waters today.*

can be traced, only a few living types extend well back into the geological record. One example is the horn shark family, Heterodontidae. Horn sharks are not found in Hawai'i but they are common along the temperate coasts of California, the Galápagos Islands, Japan, South Africa, and Australia. The fossil record of this family extends back to the lithographic limestone of the Jurassic Period, 160 million years ago. To give a perspective, this is the same fossil stratum in which the early ancestor of birds, *Archaeopteryx*, was found. Thus the shark family Heterodontidae has remained relatively unchanged (at least in its skeletal structure) for the same period in which birds have undergone substantial changes. By comparison, more highly evolved sharks, such as great whites and makos, are believed to date only to the Eocene—about 50 million years ago, the same as many coral reef fishes.

Another, now faded, myth about sharks purports that their upper jaws are rigidly fixed to their skull (or neurocranium, as shark biologists prefer to call it). This old fisherman's tale made its way into semiserious writings about sharks. Some older textbooks explained that, because of the supposed rigidity of the upper jaw attachment, sharks needed to swim upside down to take a proper bite. This misconception began to wane as soon as people began to observe sharks in their environment. In 1925, William Beebe watched from his heavy diving helmet 30 feet (9 m) under the sea at

There was a myth that sharks' jaws were rigidly fixed to their skulls. Some books even suggested that sharks could not bite properly unless they swam on their back. As this picture of the feeding great white shark indicates, the upper jaw can be extended during feeding.

Despite their fearsome reputation, great white sharks are beautiful, graceful animals.

Cocos Island off Costa Rica. He noted that sharks were much more adaptable in their behavior than had been thought.

A conclusive demonstration of the marked flexibility of the upper jaw in the great white shark has been provided by shark biologists Tim Tricas and John McCosker. They analyzed slow-motion films of feeding great white sharks taken by noted cinematographer Al Giddings and showed that the upper jaw protrudes a substantial distance during a bite. Even sharks like the California horn shark (whose diet is limited to hard-shelled animals such as sea urchins and clams) are able to protrude their jaws when engulfing a prey animal.

Basic Characteristics

A good way to review the characteristics of sharks is to contrast them with bony fishes.

Skeletal structure

The skeletons of bony fishes are structurally quite different from those of sharks. Although both sharks and bony fishes have mineralized skeletons, the amount and manner in which calcium salts are deposited in the two kinds of skeletons are very different. Bony fishes have more heavily mineralized bone tissue.

Some biologists have suggested that the reduced calcification in the skeleton of sharks might be an adaptation to decrease density, making them lighter in seawater. Bony fishes control their buoyancy with special organs called gas bladders. The volume of these internal sacs (located between the intestines and the vertebral column) can be regulated to respond to depth changes. Sharks have no such organ and must spend a lot of energy swimming or they sink to the bottom. The large liver in a shark (filled with oil that is less dense than seawater) and the lightened skeleton are both adaptations for increasing swimming efficiency.

Gill openings

Although bony fishes have at least five paired gill arches, they only have a single external gill opening on each side. The gills are protected by a bony

---

plate called an opercle, familiar to any fisherman who has removed a hook and held a bony fish by the gills. In contrast, sharks have no such bony covering. They may have up to seven external gill openings, but the usual number is five.

In addition, many sharks have a pair of openings to the gills called spiracles. In some species (e.g., the dogfish family), the spiracles are large and well developed. They are used to inhale oxygen-filled water and pass it over the gills. Lacking large spiracles, most sharks use only their mouths to inhale water. In some sharks (e.g., the cookiecutter shark), breathing can continue through the spiracle while the mouth is occupied with feeding.

Eyelids

Bony fishes cannot close their eyes. However, many kinds of sharks have an eyelid, called a nictitating membrane, that covers their eyes during feeding. Other sharks, such as great white sharks, lack such a membrane but roll their eyes inside the eye socket in the neurocranium as protection against the scratching struggles of their prey.

Scales

A very noticeable difference between most bony fishes and sharks is their skin covering. Bony fishes have overlapping scales. Sharks are covered with myriads of structures very similar to teeth, called denticles. Their shape varies over the body to help streamline the shark. The raspy, rough quality of shark skin is caused by these tiny toothlike nodes.

Fin structure

Another obvious difference between bony fishes and sharks is seen

---

A basic difference between the so-called bony fishes and the cartilaginous fishes—the sharks and rays—is the structure of their skeletons. This close-up of the margin of a tiger shark jaw shows the growing edge of cartilage. The golden brown area behind it is cartilage that has been mineralized by special calcium salts.

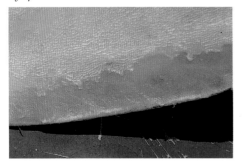

Above: *This side view of a cookiecutter shark shows the extreme protrusibility and suctorial lips used in biting cookie-shaped chunks from large fishes. Note the large eye, reduced gill slits, and the distinctive brown band around the head.*

Right: *This close-up of the eye of an adult blacktip reef shark shows a pencil point holding the partially closed eyelid, or nictitating membrane. Not all sharks have these membranes, but those that do use them to cover the eyes for protection during feeding.*

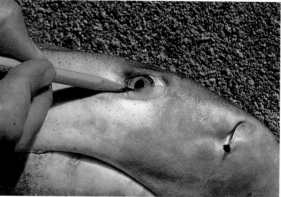

Below: *There are many differences between bony fishes and sharks (such as this salmon and this sevengill shark, a species not found in Hawai'i. It has the most gill-slits of any sharks). Although bony fishes have at least five gill arches on each side, they have a single external gill opening with a protective bony plate called an opercle. Sharks have from five to seven pairs of gill openings (depending on the species) and no bony plate.*

in the structure of fins. Sharks have broad-based, fleshy, relatively inflexible fins. In bony fishes, all fins—dorsal, anal, pelvic, pectoral, and tail—are very flexible. They are made up of a number of serial elements (called rays or spines depending on their stiffness) all under separate muscular control. Such a structure permits the use of all the fins in bony fishes as propulsive elements. For example, the *humuhumunukunukuāpua'a*, or the triggerfish, uses rapid undulations of its dorsal and anal fins to move over the reef. Sharks, with their relatively inflexible fins, are limited to the use of the tail fin as a driving force. The other fins are modifiers of this single source of propulsion. The dorsal and anal fins provide rotational stability, and the pectoral fins provide the same kind of lift and diving control as airplane wings.

Teeth

Most bony fishes have teeth in sockets of their jaws. Sharks have rows of teeth tightly but only superficially attached to the jaw. These rows grow continuously and simultaneously, thus assuring sharp replacement teeth whether or not new teeth are needed. The replacement rate of teeth varies depending on the species and size of the individual. In an adult tiger shark, for example, a new cutting row of teeth may be in place every seven to ten days. The shape of teeth is highly adapted in both fishes and sharks. Relative size and shape vary with species. Most shark teeth are distinctive enough to identify many species from only a few teeth.

Sharks have fleshy, broad-based, relatively inflexible fins. Bony fishes have complex, extremely flexible fins made up of a number of repeated parts called fin rays. Each ray has sets of muscles that erect, depress, and rotate it. Thus the fins in bony fishes can be used for locomotion and even communication through signaling.

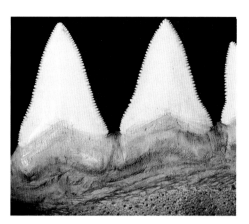

Above left: *Teeth of the mako shark. Each mako tooth is about 1 inch (2.5 cm) long. These daggerlike teeth, like all shark teeth, are arranged in replacement rows. In a living shark, they would be partially covered by tissue.*

Middle left: *The distinctive, obliquely notched, serrated teeth of tiger sharks are unique. The width across the base of this tooth is about 3/4 inch (2 cm).*

Above right: *Equally distinctive are the triangular serrated teeth of the great white shark, about an inch wide (2.5 cm) across the base in this example.*

Middle right: *Inch-long strip of tiny teeth from a 15-foot long (458 cm) whale shark.*

Right: *Here is a 1 inch (2.5 cm) band of teeth from Megamouth I. Biologists believe that the great white, the mako, and the megamouth sharks may be more closely related to one another than to other shark species. This hypothesis is based on the structure of the teeth as well as other characteristics.*

13

PHOTO BY DOC WHITE/IMAGES UNLIMITED

These two whitetip reef sharks are engaged in pre-copulatory courtship biting. The smaller male is gripping the female's pectoral fin in his teeth preparatory to entwining his body beneath hers and inserting a clasper into her cloacal opening. The sharks will sink to the bottom until copulation is complete. This species is one of the few in which actual copulation has been observed. Biologists only speculate how other large shark species mate in open water.

Sexual Reproduction

Most bony fishes broadcast their sperm and unfertilized eggs into open water, where fertilization takes place. After spending a few days in the plankton or in a nest attached to the bottom, the eggs hatch as tiny transparent fish larvae. The larvae spend several weeks in the plankton before metamorphosing into juveniles that more closely resemble the adults. There are a few exceptions to this reproductive mode in bony fishes. Surf perches (of the family Embiotocidae) give birth to miniature adults. In sea horses and pipefishes the male retains the fertilized eggs until the young hatch.

In marked contrast with most fishes, fertilization in all sharks is internal, meaning that the male and female copulate. All male sharks have paired extensions of their pelvic fins called claspers. The elongated structures are inserted (one at a time) into the female to deliver the sperm. Depending on the species of shark, the fertilized eggs are retained internally for various lengths of time, and there is a variety of ways in which the mother provides nutrition for the embryo. Some sharks (none of the inshore species in Hawai'i) lay eggs. The female deposits a variable number of eggs in rocky crevices, or attaches them by tendrils to sessile animals like seafans. Each egg case contains a single shark embryo connected by a tube to a calorie-rich yolk. Yolk and embryo are surrounded

14

by a leathery case. There is no maternal care, other than the initial selection of a safe place in which to leave the eggs.

In other species, eggs are retained inside the mother's enlarged oviducts. After the yolk is consumed, the young sharks hatch internally and are born into the water. In some forms, such as sand tiger sharks, threshers, makos, and perhaps great white sharks, an internally hatched embryo remains in the mother's oviduct, eating its later-arriving siblings in the form of eggs passing down the oviduct. With this added nutrition and no competition for space within the oviduct, the young of these species grow to a relatively

large size before entering the real world of the sea and the reef.

In most of the sharks found in the inshore waters of Hawai'i (including tiger, gray reef, blacktip reef, whitetip reef, sandbar, and hammerhead sharks), there is a tubelike physical connection (sometimes called the pseudo-umbilicus) that connects the embryo to the maternal tissue of the mother. Such a reproductive mode severely limits the number of young produced by each female. Thus, heavy fishing of sharks can reduce the population for several generations.

Above: *These four different egg cases are from four different kinds of sharks—the upper two cat sharks, the lower two horn sharks. The largest egg case is about 4 inches (10 cm). At the far right is the juvenile horn shark that hatched out of the screw-shaped egg case next to it. No shallow-water sharks in Hawai'i lay eggs.*

Below right: *This near-term gray reef pup bears a pseudo-umbilical cord that connects the young shark to maternal tissue.*

Below left: *Even a quick look of the pelvic fins of this adult 16-foot long (488 cm) great white shark leaves no doubt as to its gender.*

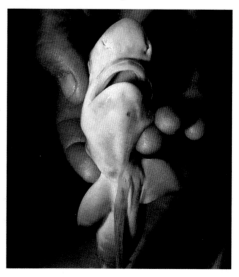

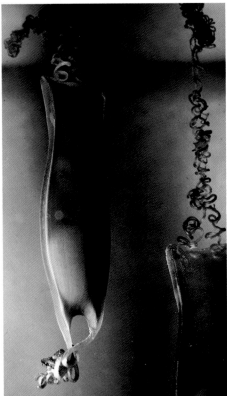

Above: *This close-up of a mature female's cloacal opening shows the paired genital papillae where the male's clasper is inserted during mating.*

Left: *This close-up of a 4-inch long (10 cm) cat shark egg case shows the nutrient-rich yellow yolk near the bottom. Midway can be seen the pale nose and dark eyes of the developing embryo. It is connected to the yolk by a tube. When this baby shark matures and has consumed all of the nutrition of the yolk, it will hatch from the flexible egg case and fend for itself as a tiny but completely developed cat shark.*

Below: *The short claspers in this young gray reef shark indicate that it is an immature male. In mature males the claspers extend well beyond the ends of the pelvic fins.*

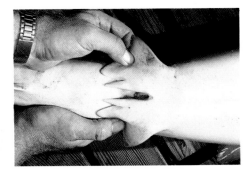

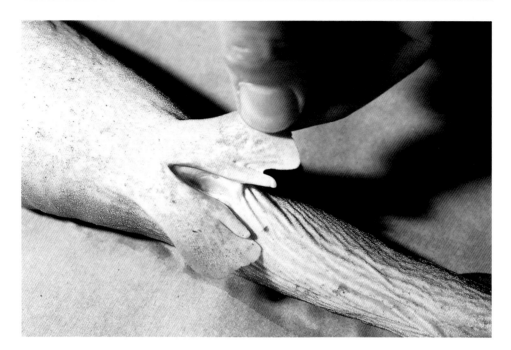

Above: *Consider these small claspers of a juvenile whale shark. In a mature male the claspers may be as long as a person's arm.*

Right: *This peppered cat shark (Galeus piperatus) is small but the elongated claspers indicate that it is a mature male. This species is not found in Hawai'i.*

Below: *The tube formed by the complex folding of this blacktip reef shark conducts sperm into the female. Also visible are hooks on the clasper tip that pierce the inner walls of the female's oviduct to assure a successful coupling.*

Sharks and Hawaiian Culture

Sharks were viewed in complex ways by Hawaiians. Before contact with the West, shark teeth provided their most frequently used cutting edge, functioning as a knife. Shark skins were used for the membrane of temple and hula drums of large size. Most important, because of their dangerous nature, some sharks were considered to be the equal of high *ali'i*, and to some, *ali'i* was attributed the dangerous, devouring nature of sharks.

Although shark meat from certain species was occasionally to rarely eaten by men, it was forbidden to women because of the association of sharks with religious concepts of *kapu*, power, and high *ali'i* status.

Carcharhinus amblyrhynchos
(gray reef shark)
This imaginative painting combines traditions of Hawaiian culture and gray reef shark biology. Large aggregations of adult female gray reef sharks seasonally visit the shallow reefs of Laysan Island and other places in the unpopulated northwestern Hawaiian Islands. Their dorsal fins and tails break the surface and dozens to hundreds of sharks can be counted at one time.

Ancient Hawaiian legends tell of shark-keepers, kahu manō, *who cared for individual shark 'aumakua. There are also heiau near the shoreline that are said to be locations sharks visited. Perhaps many years ago when the nearshore waters of Hawai'i were not crowded with noisy boats, large aggregations of gray reef sharks visited the high-island reef flats just as they do today in the northwestern Hawaiian Islands. Perhaps Hawaiian people who had sharks as 'aumakua waded or swam among them without harm, communing with the serene grace of this beautiful and powerful animal.*

Sharks as Spiritual Figures

Some sharks were revered as influential spirits important to a geographic area like Pearl Harbor or Hālawa Valley. Others were more limited in their influence and were special to particular families or individuals. The Hawaiians believed that under certain conditions, sometimes with the assistance of surviving family members, a deceased relative was reincarnated in the form of a shark—not any shark, but a specific shark known by a special name.

Such a shark could be an *'aumakua*—a beneficent guardian spirit, a family protector, a fishing helper—or an *'unihipili*—a spirit that would do the bidding, for ill or for good, of its sorcerer-caretaker. *'Aumākua* were the more prevalent form. Sometimes an *'aumakua* was brought forth with the help of a *kahuna*; sometimes they appeared unbidden. There were also *'aumākua* in the form of other animals besides sharks. These included owls, mudhens, sea turtles, eels, caterpillars (and their marine counterparts, sea cucumbers), even rocks and plants.

In 1870, Kamakau recorded a method by which an *'aumakua* could be brought forth from the remains of a dead family member:

> The *kahu manō* (shark keeper, either a relative or a *kahuna*) took *'awa* at dawn and at dusk

for two or three days, until he saw clearly that the body had definitely assumed the form of a shark...with recognizable marks (of the deceased) on the cheeks or sides, like a tattoo or an earring mark. After two or three days more, when the *kahu manō* saw the strengthening of this new shark...he sent for the relatives...[so they could]...see with their own eyes that the deceased had become a shark, with all the signs by which they could not fail to recognize the loved one in a deep ocean. If the relatives should go bathing or fishing in the sea, it would come around and they would all recognize the markings of their own shark. It became their defender in the sea. (quoted in Pukui et al., 1972, p. 116–117)

Mary Kawena Pukui related a similar version in *Nānā i ke Kumu* (a book based on interviews with Hawaiians in a collaborative program of the Hawaiian Culture Committee of the Queen Lili'uokalani Children's Center):

> The bones were wrapped in tapa...then the family would go down to the sea and pray and give offerings (food and *'awa*). Then, it was believed, the shark would come and take this bundle of bones right under its pectoral fin. The shark would hold the bones there. Then for a while the family would

---

Whitetip reef sharks commonly seek shelter under deep reef overhangs and are often found in pairs or groups in reef caves. Although this species may not be the most abundant shark in Hawai'i, it is probably the one most commonly seen by divers and snorklers. A whitetip is a docile, harmless shark as long as it is left alone.

Their strong gill muscles enable them to pump water over their gills while they rest. Individual whitetips have been observed to live in the same caves and reef area up to at least ten years. Such loyalty to an area may have reinforced the Hawaiian belief in 'aumākua.

PHOTO BY JOHN E. RANDALL

keep coming back with offerings, until the bundle of bones took the form of a shark. (Pukui et al.,1972, p. 116)

An increasing number of sport divers are flirting with danger and questionable ethics by hand-feeding whitetip reef sharks.

The family could "name the fish you want and [the shark] will bring it back. The family can never be drowned…the shark appears and the men ride on its back" (Beckwith, as quoted in Pukui et al., 1972, p. 37).

What species of sharks were 'aumākua? Few people today can speak with authority on this question that combines taxonomy with spirituality. As a biologist, with a deep respect for the Hawaiian culture and race, I can only suggest some possibilities based on observations and on the writings of Hawaiian scholars.

Some individual sharks, like whitetip reef sharks, are known to frequent the same caves for years at a time. They are docile and relatively harmless to humans but have all the

predatory power of big sharks. Today, divers hand-feed them regularly. Such feeding is for sport and is not imbued with religious feeling.

Larger, more aggressive sharks (qualities one might also welcome in an 'aumakua) occur predictably in specific areas. Further, they form groupings and interact socially. Such behavior might have influenced the Hawaiian perspective about them.

Aggregations of carcharhinoid sharks have been reported for a number of species including the gray reef, Galapagos, sandbar, and hammerhead sharks. These groupings appear to be motivated by reasons other than feeding and are less transitory than the crowds observed in "feeding frenzies." Some biologists suggest that such packs

21

might be related to migration or "social wandering." In 1978, Richard Johnson reported what he termed "packing behavior" in the gray reef sharks of the Marshall Islands and Tahiti. His tagging studies indicated that individual sharks remained in contact with other sharks for periods of up to three years. Although I have observed such packing behavior in a number of Pacific locations (Enewetak Atoll, Canton Island, Necker Island, Maro Reef, Pearl and Hermes Reef, Midway Islands), no such behavior has been reported in the major Hawaiian Islands. This may be due to a reduction in numbers resulting from extensive fishing.

Ancient Hawaiian legends, however, suggest that shallow-water aggregations of carcharhinoid sharks may have been common around the major Hawaiian Islands group. Special shrines (*heiau*) were constructed near the shoreline for the purpose of sacrifice to sharks, which were believed to gather seasonally (Anonymous, 1976).

In 1977–1980, with the help of biologists Patti and Brian Johnson, I studied large shallow-water gatherings of gray reef sharks in the northwestern Hawaiian Islands in the waters of the Hawaiian Islands National Wildlife

These female gray reef sharks, probably pregnant, are part of a pack of dozens of sharks that gather seasonally in the shallow waters off Laysan Island. Such aggregations have been seen at other areas in the unpopulated northwestern Hawaiian Islands. They may have occurred in the high islands before things got so busy.

Refuge, established in part to protect the population of rare Hawaiian monk seals. Our observations were made incidental to a long-term study of the ecology and behavior of the seals. The sharks were easily visible from shore as they circled in the shallow channels within the reef and exposed their backs, dorsal fins and tails above the surface. Pukui and Elbert used the perfect phrase in the *Hawaiian Dictionary* to describe this sight. *Lālani kalalea* means "protruding line (of dorsal fins of sharks above the water)." The numbers of sharks in these groups ranged from 2 to 4 in March to 68 to 171 in June.

After watching these large groups, we noticed that green sea turtles and monk seals swam through the multitude with little if any interaction with the sharks. Bruce Carlson of the Waikiki Aquarium and I decided to venture into the shallow water for a closer look.

Snorkeling observations of the sharks indicated that they were all adult female gray reef sharks swimming slowly in circles, frequently exposing the upper parts of their bodies. Although individual sharks seemingly were oblivious to persons swimming

"Lālani kalalea" certainly describes these dorsal fins of gray reef sharks aggregating over the shallow reef flat at Laysan Island.

in the water, they swam off rapidly if approached. We could not get close enough to spear one. Baited hooks were also unsuccessful; all bait was ignored by the sharks, which were apparently in a non-feeding mode. Two specimens were collected with harpoons from an inflatable outboard skiff anchored in their midst. Both sharks were pregnant with embryos in the early stages of development and possessed large livers composing 13% of their body weight. The two sharks had notably dark to black backs, unlike the lighter-colored gray reef sharks caught in deeper waters. This pigmentation faded after death to the lighter coloration generally found in this species.

Water temperatures in the shallow reef waters where the sharks swam were 1.0° to 1.5°C warmer than those at 35 feet (10 m) deep in adjacent reef

areas where gray reef sharks usually occur. The following tentative hypothesis is presented as a possible explanation for the observed aggregation:

The adult female gray reef sharks appear to have been behaving in a way that would result in an increase in body temperature. The shallow-water reef areas are warmer than the adjacent waters in which gray reef sharks are usually found. The sharks were swimming with their dark backs out of the water. They occurred in greatest abundance during times of maximum sunlight, between 11 a.m. and 3 p.m. from

This yolk and tiny developing embryo were not contained in an egg case, but were removed from a gray reef shark. This embryo is perhaps eight months from full development and would have remained connected to the nutrition-providing tissue of its mother until birth.

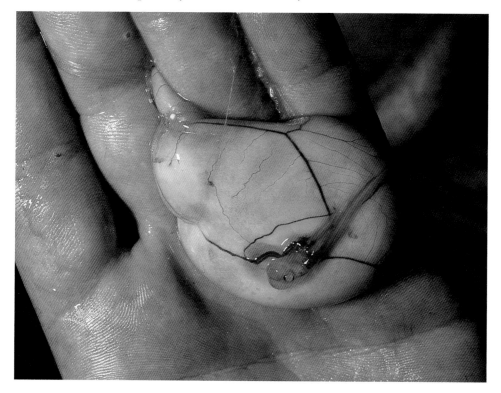

May through August. The result of an increase in body temperature could be a shortened time of development for the young and, hence, a shorter period of fasting for the pregnant female. Segregation of pregnant females from other members of the population is well documented in a number of shark species.

It is possible that such grouping behavior is not exhibited by all segments of the Hawaiian population of *Carcharinus amblyrhynchos*. In the high islands, individual gray reef sharks are known to use the same reefs for up to three years. Perhaps the contemporary Laysan population of sharks continues a behavioral pattern that is gone in the major Hawaiian Islands because of disturbances from inshore boating and fishing. Perhaps, centuries ago, such *lālani kalalea* inspired Hawaiians to

look upon gray reef sharks as very special animals.

What about contemporary Hawaiians? What are their attitudes about the sacredness of some sharks? Summarizing interviews at Queen Lili'uokalani Children's Center, Pukui reported that "for the majority of this present multicultural population, the *'aumākua* are forgotten or were never known." For some, according to Mary Pukui, *'aumakua* is a still vivid childhood memory. A middle-aged businesswoman remembers going out with her father to feed shark *'aumakua*. She added that "Hawaiians didn't go around talking about their *'aumakua*" (Pukui et al., 1972, p. 41).

The Kohala shark stone in the Bishop Museum, Honolulu, may commemorate a great white shark.

PHOTO COURTESY OF BISHOP MUSEUM

After a young surfer was killed by a large shark, probably a tiger, off West Oʻahu in November 1992, the Hawaiʻi State Department of Land and Natural Resources continued an intermittent "shark control program" designed to catch and remove large sharks from recreational areas. Despite the grief over the young man's death, the community was divided over the propriety of such fishing. As newspaper articles and editorials reflected, most people were in favor of removing large sharks. Others held the opinion that the sharks were living in their ocean (a disturbed sea at that, because of human carelessness) and humans entered the water at their own risk.

The complexity of attitudes and the practices of ancient Hawaiʻi still echo in the words of contemporary Hawaiians. Rona Kaaehuahiwi, canoe coach, was quoted in the *Honolulu Advertiser* (November 7, 1992) regarding objections that the captured sharks might be someone's *ʻaumākua*: "Those things went out with Kamehameha. What kind of books are they reading? Let it be one of their children." Buffalo Keaulana, a famous surfer and popular lifeguard on the Waiʻanae coast of Oʻahu, said, "We respect the sharks but we should fish for them where there is an attack." Asked about *ʻaumākua*, Keaulana said that he feels the idea is outmoded in places other than Niʻihau, where people maintain a more traditional relationship with the ocean. However, many older Hawaiians, especially those who are not strong Christians, still know their *ʻaumākua* and admit to saying prayers to them. The Kohala shark stone in the Bishop Museum is a tangible reminder of a legendary Hawaiian response to shark attack (see p. 42).

Hawaiian Names and Terms for Sharks

When we write about sharks in English, we can convey varying degrees of precision depending on the terms we use and their context. Scientific names (e.g., *Galeocerdo cuvier*) certainly provide the greatest precision, but well-established common names (e.g., tiger shark) can also give specific detail. Other unestablished or unqualified common names (e.g., sand shark, hammerhead shark) may denote a certain group of species but do not provide specific information.

Terms such as "the shark" and "sharks" are general to the point of vagueness. Careless use of such indefinite terms can be misleading. "Sharks are dangerous to humans" is not necessarily a true statement. "Sharks are color blind" is also false because it implies that all sharks lack color sensitivity.

Our knowledge of the shark names used by ancient Hawaiians is incomplete and spotty. It is likely that their dependence on the sea and extensive familiarity with ocean life inspired a set of specific terms for many shark species. Thirty-four species are recorded from Hawaiʻi by modern biologists. Pukui and Elbert (1971) listed nine kinds of shark in the *Hawaiian Dictionary*. Although it is likely that some species may have been unknown to Hawaiians (e.g., deep-sea forms and perhaps cookiecutter sharks, megamouth sharks, etc.), it is also probable that many of the names they used are now lost. The folk taxonomy of sharks is poorly recorded and not well understood. I would be grateful if readers with special knowledge of Hawaiian cultural relationship to sharks would

Hawaiian Gods Associated with Sharks

(Extracted from Supplement 2 of the *Hawaiian Dictionary*:
Glossary of Hawaiian gods, demigods, family gods, and a
few heroes.)

Kamohoali'i

Pele's older and favorite brother, the "most celebrated of…ancestral
shark gods" who accompanied Pele from Kahiki to Hawai'i. He
had a human form as well as shark and *hilu* fish forms.

Ka'ahupāhau

Chiefess of the shark gods of Pu'uloa (Pearl Harbor) who protected
O'ahu from sharks. She and her brother, Kahi'uka (the smiting
tail), were born as humans; she was a redhead (*'ehu*). Later they
were changed into sharks. On one occasion a girl who had snatched
an *'ilima* lei from her attendant (*kahu*) was dragged under the water
by sharks and drowned. Ka'ahupāhau vowed that never again
would sharks attack humans at Pu'uloa. The 'Ewa people fed her
and scraped barnacles off her back and her brother's. [The U.S.
Government began to develop Pearl Harbor as a naval base in 1908.
A major feature was a graving dry dock 1,800 feet long and 100 feet
wide (550 x 30 m). Dredging and construction began in 1909 in an
area long associated with the shark god. When the unfinished
structure collapsed into wreckage in February 1913, Hawaiians
reminded engineers that Ka'ahupāhau had not been propitiated.
Today's dry docks in Pearl Harbor are still not at peace with
sharks. Numerous juvenile hammerheads, born in Pearl Harbor
in the spring months, are left high and dry within the docks as
water is pumped out.]

Kaehuikimanō-o-Pu'uloa

(Lit. the little shark redhead of Pearl Harbor.) A shark god of
Puna, Hawai'i, born of humans at Pānau, Puna. He was named for
the redhead (*'ehu*) of Ka'ahupāhau, chiefess of Pearl Harbor shark
gods. He was reared on kava mixed with mother's milk.

Kaholia-Kāne

A shark god of Kalaniopu'u, a ruling chief of Hawai'i at the time
of Kamehameha. The shark lived in a cave at Puhi, Kaua'i.

Kāne'āpua

A trickster *kupua* described variously as a brother of Pele, as a bird brother of Namaka-o-Kaha'i, as a younger shark brother of Kāne and Kanaloa, and as a fish god of Kaunolū, Lāna'i, where a nearby islet is named for him. He angered Kāne and Kanaloa by urinating in their water, and they flew away as birds. Wahanui (great mouth), a voyager bound for Kahiki, passed Kaunolū Point and Kāne'āpua hailed him. Wahanui replied that his canoe was full, but when Kāne raised a storm, he took Kāne'āpua aboard. Kāne'āpua quieted two *kupua* hills, Paliuli (dark cliff) and Palikea (white cliff), that clashed together, destroying canoes, and he performed many other feats. On the journey of the Pele family from Kahiki, Pele's brother Kamohoali'i abandoned Kāne'āpua on Nihoa Island. Later Pele longed for him and Kamohoali'i steered back to rescue him.

Kawelomahamahai'a

An older brother of Kawelo, who was turned into a shark and was worshiped.

Keali'ikau-o-Ka'ū

A shark god who protected the Ka'ū people from sharks. He was a cousin of Pele and the son of Kua. He had an affair with a young human of Waikapuna, Ka'ū, and she gave birth to a beneficent green shark.

Kua

A shark god called the king shark of Ka'ū and the ancestor of numerous Ka'ū folk. With Kaholia-Kāne he raised a storm between Kaua'i and O'ahu to prevent the marriage of their divine relative, Pele, and Lohi'au, a mortal. His full name may have been Kua'a-Wākea.

Kūhaimoana

A shark god, brother of Pele, who lived at Ka'ula Islet, where he was left when the Pele family migrated from Kahiki to Hawai'i. He was said to be thirty fathoms long and to be the husband of Ka'ahupāhau. He was also called Kūheimoana (lit. Kū following ocean).

correct, confirm, or augment the deductions and speculations made in this chapter.

It is careless, inaccurate, and perhaps even irresponsible for modern commentators to make such imprecise statements as "sharks are sacred to Hawaiians" and "Hawaiians did not kill sharks" or "sharks were important food for Hawaiians." Such statements are true for some species, but we are by no means certain which species match which Hawaiian names.

However, we can speculate and make informed guesses by reviewing Hawaiian records about sharks and by comparing the attitudes they reflect with contemporary knowledge of shark biology and surviving oral tradition. Such informed guessing should only be done with care and should clearly be identified as speculation. Yet there is an unfortunate tendency among contemporary spokespeople to use imprecise "knowledge" of Hawaiian tradition to influence others. For example, after a fatal shark attack on Maui in 1991, a local radio personality

This replica duplicates an artifact in the Bishop Museum that was used in hand-to-hand combat in ancient Hawai'i. It features the sharp cutting edges of tiger shark teeth lashed to strong sennit cord. A thumb and fourth finger fit through each loop, arming the fist with a lethal cutting edge.

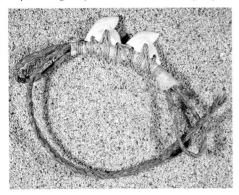

inflamed a segment of public opinion about a state-supported fishing program aimed at removing large and dangerous tiger sharks from the area of the attack. He claimed that to do so would be tantamount to "killing our ancestors." Others stated that the ancient Hawaiians did not kill sharks because "they were sacred." As we shall see, ancient Hawaiian culture was complex in its consideration of sharks and recognized that different kinds were to be treated in special ways unique to each species and, in some cases, unique to individual sharks.

The Hawaiian language, like modern English, used a general term for sharks when appropriate. Pukui and Elbert (1986) listed this general term as *manō*. It is applied in a variety of contexts to refer to sharks as a group. Examples include aphorisms such as *"pau pele, pau manō,"* an oath similar to the English "cross my heart and hope to die [if what I say is not true]." Pukui and Elbert translated this Hawaiian pledge as "consumed by volcanic fire; consumed by shark [may I die if I don't keep my pledge]".

In English we call lecherous young men "wolves" but Pukui and Elbert recorded that the Hawaiian language refers to them as "sharks." *Ho'omanō* is "to behave like a shark; to pursue women ardently." Weapons made from various kinds of shark teeth are called *leiomano*. Pukui and Elbert suggested that this word may be based on *lei o manō*, "a shark's lei."

Manō is also used in Hawaiian with qualifiers to make it a more specific term, just as English does with, for instance, "great white shark," and "scalloped hammerhead shark."

Pukui and Elbert translated *manō pā'ele* as "black-smudged shark."

Perhaps this refers to the distinctive black marks on the dorsal fins of a relatively common inshore Hawaiian species whose markings are also noted in its English common name, blacktip reef shark, and its scientific name, *Carcharhinus melanopterus*. The less common deeper-water species, *C. limbatus*, the blacktip shark, also has distinctively marked fins.

Pukui and Elbert record the name *manō 'ula*, or "red shark." There is no red-colored shark species in Hawai'i. However, they noted that red is a sacred color in Hawai'i. Perhaps this term was reserved for special sharks. They also stated that *'ula* (meaning red) was a shortened term for *koa'e'ula*, the red-tailed tropic bird. Is it possible that the markedly elongated tail of thresher sharks (*Alopias* spp.) reminded Hawaiians of the distinctive long, slender tail of tropic birds?

In *Place Names of Hawaii*, Pukui et al. (1974) cited several locations with *manō* in the name. It is not clear today which

Leiomano is the Hawaiian name for weapons made from shark teeth. This circle of shark teeth in a typical blunt-nosed tiger shark suggests a much different image than the more welcomed garland of flowers.

species may be involved. However, it is likely that the Hawaiians referred to a specific kind of shark, given the elaborate legends associated with the places. It is also possible that a name implied no specific shark but rather intended the idea of sharks in general.

In the Hālawa area of Moloka'i, the name for the land section of *Kaimumanō* translates literally as "the shark oven." Pukui and Elbert recounted the story of a cannibal shark-man, Nanaue, who was caught at Kainalu and dragged up the gulch and hill. His body left a shallow ravine, and near the top of *Pu'umanō* (shark hill) there is a rock with a deeply cut groove entirely around it. The people cut up Nanaue with sharp bamboo and burned his flesh.

Whale sharks are noted for their docility and hospitality to divers.

On Oʻahu, in upper Kamana Nui Valley, is a ridge named *Manō*. Legend tells of a shark-man who lived in a cave there. Both shark and man were known as *Keanaokamanō* (the cave of the shark). The man followed swimmers to the sea and killed them, but he was finally killed himself by the victims' families. Hawaiian stories of men (*manō kanaka*) who transformed into murdering sharks are suggestive of European legends of werewolves (enchanted men who transformed into wolflike killers). Both are based on fearsome predators.

Other Hawaiian shark names do not involve *manō*, just as English common names do not always contain the word shark. Of the extant Hawaiian shark names, only a few can be fairly certainly matched with scientific names.

The *Hawaiian Dictionary* (1971) defines *lālākea* (literally, white fins) as "reef shark or Hawaiian dogfish [sic]; four to six feet long, gray with lighter colored fins; considered harmless." This description closely fits the white-tip reef shark, *Triaenodon obesus*. Beckley described *lālākea* as having white fins, and reported that these sharks were "caught in old nets…the large ones by hooks" (as quoted in Buck, 1964, p. 288) for food. The mention of the use of "old nets" also supports the contention that *lālākea* is the whitetip reef shark. This species tends to hide in caves and stay close to the bottom—habits that ensure the snagging and tearing of nets.

Kamakau (1976) listed *lele waʻa* as one of the basic kinds of sharks. Pukui and Elbert suggested that the name referred to "the friendly shark that was said to lean on canoe outriggers for food and company." In the absence of other information about which species may be involved, we must speculate about Pukui's and Elbert's remarks. Certainly the "friendliest" shark in Hawaiian waters is the whale shark, *Rhincodon typus*. This largest of all fish (reliably reported to reach a length of 35 feet [1,067 cm]) eats small schooling fishes and plankton. Harmless and docile, whale sharks often permit swimmers and divers to grab their fins and hitch rides as the large sharks cruise along. Whale sharks in the wild and in aquariums (e.g., Okinawa Expo Aquarium and Osaka Ring of Fire Aquarium) learn to approach boats and catwalks where food is delivered by the bucketful (or calabashful) into their broad mouths. Although they do not jump (as *lele* might suggest), whale sharks are as large as outrigger and double-hulled canoes (*waʻa*).

The *Hawaiian Dictionary* also defines a similar word, *lele waʻa*, as "transferring

This 20-foot (610 cm) whale shark lives in a 2-million-gallon (6,500 ton) aquarium in Osaka, Japan. It is shown here approaching the aquarists' catwalk for feeding. Note the bucket that is dumping shrimp in front of the whale shark's mouth.

at sea from canoe to canoe or canoe to surfboard for the sport of surfing to shore" (literally, canoe leaping). Perhaps ancient Hawaiians, encountering a docile whale shark at the surface, leaped from their canoe to its canoe-sized back, to catch an exciting ride just as modern divers and snorkelers do.

Niuhi: A Fierce Predator

What names did the Hawaiians award to such abundant and dynamic species as *Carcharhinus amblyrhynchos*, the gray reef shark; *Carcharhinus plumbeus*, the sandbar shark; and *Galeocerdo cuvier*, the tiger shark? And what shark species is the *niuhi*—clearly a most fearsome species? Is it the tiger shark, as some authors suggest? Could it be the great white shark? Only Handy and Pukui (in their important book, *The Polynesian Family System in Ka'u, Hawaii*, 1972) say that it is—and oddly, Pukui does not repeat that definition in her original dictionary.

Perhaps, like *manō*, *niuhi* referred to

both species of dangerous sharks in Hawai'i, the tiger and the great white. Yet it seems unlikely that Hawaiians, so precise with other names for animals, did not differentiate between these two very different, large, dangerous animals. Very probably they did distinguish them. Literate reporters of oral tradition have probably confused both species under a single surviving name, and the other is now lost.

The two largest, most dangerous sharks in Hawai'i are the great white (remember *Jaws*?) and the tiger. The pair, both associated with fatalities of swimmers, have almost as many differences as similarities. As adults, both species commonly reach 15–18 feet long (457–549 cm). Tigers occur fairly commonly in Hawaiian waters and range in size from newborn 18-inch (46 cm) pups to adults that exceed the length of the largest old-style surfboards. In research fishing programs conducted in Hawai'i in 1977–1978, 28 tigers were landed ranging in length from 4 to 15 feet (122–457 cm) and averaging almost 8 feet (244 cm) long.

In contrast, great white sharks occur only rarely in Hawai'i and apparently only as adults. A search of records back to 1886 revealed only eight confirmed reports or landings of great white sharks in Hawai'i. These rare encounters with humans were diverse and noteworthy. It is likely that the ancient Hawaiians had equally notable and perhaps even more varied experiences with this large and dangerous species. The teeth of great whites were used in Hawaiian tools and weapons.

Whether a given species is rare or common now, it is highly likely that all sharks were more abundant in ancient Hawai'i. Today's high population, heavy fishing, and extensive disturbance to nearshore waters take their toll on all the organisms in Hawaiian seas. There is some evidence that sharks are more abundant in the uninhabited (but increasingly fished) northwestern Hawaiian Islands.

To give an idea of relative abundance, commercial fishermen often report the "number of fish caught per number of hooks set." In research fishing programs in the Hawaiian archipelago, catch rate has exceeded 3 tiger sharks per 100 hooks, reflecting a fair abundance of tigers. As a part of some shark fishing programs, the State has promoted tiger shark meat (as well as that of other species) as a product for home and restaurant consumption. Initial resistance to tiger shark steaks was soon overcome when restaurateurs and fish market operators tasted well-handled and well-prepared shark at a variety of free dinners and pupu parties. Shark-related souvenirs are also popular in island novelty shops.

The problem with shark fisheries is the sharp decline in catch rate with sustained effort. After an initial high yield, the catch of sharks drops dramatically. This effect is desirable if the intent is to reduce the number of sharks in an area; this has been the main purpose of the State's "shark reduction programs" that have usually followed a well-publicized human attack. However, this rapid decrease in numbers with heavy fishing makes it difficult to maintain a dependable fishery.

The powerful tail of the great white shark can propel it out of the water during a feeding bout.

PHOTO BY ROSEMARY CHASTNEY / IMAGES UNLIMITED

Although Hawaiians before Captain Cook's arrival fished for sharks, even with the highest of estimated population figures for the ancient Hawaiians it is unlikely that shark populations were markedly reduced, although their numbers must certainly have been affected.

The reason shark populations are so sensitive to heavy fishing lies in their reproductive biology. Unlike most fishes, which release hundreds of thousands of eggs into the sea, sharks give birth to very few young. A mother tiger shark may deliver a litter of small (12–18 inches [30–46 cm]) pups numbering in the dozens.

By contrast, a great white shark of the same size gives birth to one or two pups perhaps 4 feet long (122 cm). These two species play different sides of the biological gaming table: by producing a greater number of smaller young, the tiger shark enhances the chances that several young will survive. On the other hand, the larger size at birth of great white shark pups gives them a head start in a hard world.

We know from artifact and story that the ancient Hawaiians actively fished for sharks for food, for teeth to be used as the cutting edges of tools and weapons, for skin to stretch as drum heads, and for ceremonial purposes. Lacking metal, Hawaiian shark fishermen (and they were fisher*men* because such fishing was *kapu* for women) used large wooden hooks tipped with whale bone; leaders and lines were heavy, braided sennit.

Recall the scene in the feature film *Jaws*: the trio of shark fishermen had a powerful motor vessel, stainless steel harpoons, floats made from metal drums, and other diverse technological accessories. Even in the real world of

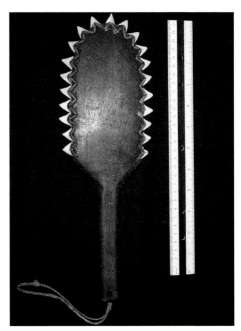

This heavy koa war-club was collected by George Vancouver on a subsequent trip to Hawai'i after he served abroad Cook's voyages of discovery. The war-club is ringed with great white shark teeth.

documentary films, great white sharks are hunted with very heavy-duty specialized gear.

Compare that equipment with the gear available to a band of Hawaiian fishermen in old Hawai'i. Their struggle to subdue an adult great white shark with rope made from plant fiber while braced in a wooden canoe must have been rigorous indeed. Great white sharks are strong, active animals that seriously resist capture. Large tigers are also no easy matter to land but they seem to lose their will to win quickly compared with great white sharks. Filmmakers have successfully exploited "fished-out" tigers and drafted them as tractable actors in feature films.

Although great white sharks are rare in Hawai'i, their occasional visits here have understandably been of

human interest whether before or after the arrival of Captain Cook. In May 1926, a 12½-foot (380 cm) specimen was caught by fishermen off Kahuku, O'ahu; its stomach contained human remains. At Mākaha, O'ahu, in March 1969, a great white shark attacked a surfboard, resulting in a frightened

Left: *Long-line fishing techniques are used by both commercial fishermen and the periodic "shark-control programs" designed to remove large sharks from nearshore waters. Arrayed on the deck of this commercial fishing boat are the coiled lines and large hooks baited with tuna used to catch tiger sharks up to 16 feet long (488 cm).*

Below: *Most of what is known about Hawaiian sharks has been learned through the study of dead specimens. Laudable efforts are now under way to learn about living sharks in their natural environment. Here, a marine biologist takes a measurement of a Hawaiian sandbar shark.*

surfer with a lacerated calf and a stronger love of the land, and distinct triangular tooth impressions in the board. The attacker swam away, but its identity was confirmed by biologists who examined the typical shape of the tooth fragments and impressions.

Great white sharks are most commonly found along continental coasts in temperate waters, especially where seals and sea lions are abundant. Such areas include South Africa, southern Australia, and the Pacific and Atlantic coasts of North and South America. The usual food of great white sharks of the size caught in Hawai'i is seals and sea lions. Attacks on these animals by great white sharks are frequently witnessed and recorded by biologists working at the Farallon Islands just off San Francisco's Golden Gate.

The high islands of Hawai'i do not have a resident seal population, but a small population of endangered Hawaiian monk seals survives in the northwestern Hawaiian Islands. No one has yet reported tangible evidence that seals ever occurred in the main islands, although in recent years, stragglers from the northwest have been sighted on Kaua'i, O'ahu, Maui, and Hawai'i.

Recent work on Hawaiian midden material and on fossil birds suggests that colonizing Polynesians may have rapidly exterminated defenseless species such as flightless birds and perhaps large colonies of monk seals. It may be possible that great white sharks were more abundant in Hawai'i during a period when monk seals may have colonized the main islands. We do know that Hawaiians were using great white shark teeth in tools and weapons before Cook's arrival.

Great white sharks very probably

A healthy sense of humor is among the many attitudes from which to consider sharks in Hawai'i. This shark souvenir item from the Waikiki Aquarium was a best seller.

influenced a number of legends in Hawaiian tradition. One major feature of a successful dominator of any environment is keen eyesight. Great white sharks possess excellent vision and are one of the few sharks we know to have color vision.

Hawaiian legend recounts that during her pregnancy, Kamehameha's mother was struck by an intense longing to eat the eye of the *niuhi* and the rare dish was provided for her. It was later said that the keen vision of Kamehameha's leadership was influenced by the shark's spirit.

Another less successful Hawaiian chief, Kiwala'ō, a fellow warrior of Kamehameha, also sought strength from the great white sharks. His feather cloak (now in the Bishop Museum) is boldly decorated with a series of five equilateral triangles, a motif repre-

PHOTO BY AL GIDDINGS/IMAGES UNLIMITED

This 2-foot long (61 cm) tiger shark was born only days before this photograph was taken. The shark closely resembles much larger adults. The color pattern from which the species partially gets its name is much more obvious in juveniles than in adults.

senting an abstraction of shark teeth, the fierceness of the predator being associated with the wearer of the cloak. The design of equilateral triangles is strongly suggestive of the adult teeth of the fierce and powerful great white sharks. A similar pattern is found in the Elgin feather cloak and in complex tattoo motifs.

For sheer practical reasons the equilateral shape of great white sharks teeth makes excellent cutting edges for weapons and tools. Adult teeth are thick, and the broad base gives added strength to the tooth. In a survey of tools and weapons collected on Captain Cook's voyages and now distributed among several world museums, I

found eight implements that utilize great white shark teeth. Anthropologists generally assume that the artifacts collected on Cook's trips were made before the Hawaiian culture was influenced by Western tradition.

We know only some of the uses that Hawaiians had for shark teeth. The teeth presented the sharpest and thinnest edge that they had to cut designs into *kapa* bamboo stampers, wooden *kapa* beaters, decorative bases and elements of drums and gourds. Teeth fastened to heavy wooden clubs were extremely damaging weapons. Daggers had their edges lined with shark teeth. Some writers have suggested that these were eviscerators used in hand-to-hand combat to deliver a mortal blow to the opponent's midsection.

I have held these implements, and they fit the hand in at least three positions. Perhaps they were used as weapons, but one can also imagine that they were highly valued as tools for detailed carving. The shape of the tooth of the great white sharks makes a particularly efficient tool from an engineering sense, but it is possible that the broad-based triangle was also a motif associated with spiritual power. I have examined two post-Cook implements that are very similar to the pre-Cook tools containing genuine great white shark teeth. However, these two later articles were made with whale bone and iron in shapes that resemble a great white shark tooth. In fact, the whale bone was even notched on the margin to resemble dental serrations. Although these may have been crude attempts by Western owners to replace a lost genuine tooth, I prefer to think that they represent the *mana* of the great white shark combined with other significant materials.

Above: *This fist weapon was collected during one of the expeditions of Captain James Cook. The teeth are probably from a gray reef shark.*

Below: *Ancient Hawaiians actively fished for large sharks. Hooks (called* kīholo) *were carefully and strongly crafted from wood or bone. This replica of an artifact at the Bishop Museum was made by craftsman-anthropologist Tony Maiava. It accurately represents the complex connection of the sennit leader and the hook's sharp tip of whale bone.*

PHOTO BY TOM KELLY

As significant as the great white shark must have been in Hawaiian culture, the more abundant and equally large tiger shark may have been more important. Tiger shark teeth are certainly more common in tools and weapons: in knives, fist weapons, heavy clubs, and light wooden scepters. Their semi-circular, obliquely notched shape is unique and distinctively different from that of any other species. Just as the tooth shape differs from that of great white sharks, so do the tiger shark's behavior and habits.

Tigers are famous for their indiscriminate palate. Adults take floating seabirds and sleeping turtles and poke their blunt noses into caves to pull out lobsters. Modern tigers are renowned for eating garbage. Reportedly, tigers have been caught with trash can lids in their stomachs (for an example see the Register of Shark Attacks, case 18).

Presumably, the tiger sharks in Kamehameha's day were no different. It seems unlikely that such an animal (even a large individual) would have been imbued with the same mystical power and strength as that attributed to the great white shark.

Various interpreters and repeaters of Hawaiian legends have called the large dangerous sharks of Hawai'i

Hawaiian monk seals frequent the same shallow reefs as tiger sharks—also hunting for lobsters.

niuhi. However, it is seldom clear which large species is meant, the tiger or the great white. Frequently, I think, the two species have been confused in stories. But, based on the differences in the two animals, we can make some educated guesses about which species is which.

For example, Kamakau (1976, pp. 87–88) told of a special method of fishing for *niuhi*:

A fisherman sailed far out on the ocean until the land looked level with the sea, that was the place for shark fishing. When all was ready, the prow of the canoe was turned into the current so that the upswell of the current would be behind the canoe. The net containing the decomposed pig mixed with pebbles and broken kukui nut shells was tied to the starboard side of the canoe at the forward boom. Then the net was splashed into the sea and poked with a stick until the grease ran through the pebbles and shells. A shark would scent the grease, his dorsal fin would break through the surface of the sea, and it would snap its teeth close to the canoe. The large sharks were the *niuhi*; they could be tamed like pet pigs and be tickled and patted on the head. The fisherman would pat the shark on the head until it became used to being touched. Then he rested his

The head of this Hawaiian hula drum is made from the dried skin of a tiger shark.

chin on the head of the shark and slipped a noose over its head with his hands, turning his palms away from the shark lest it see their whiteness and turn and bite them. When the snare reached the gills, the fisherman eased it downward to the center of the body and tightened the noose. If it were a big shark there would be a furious tugging and battling.

It seems likely that the large *niuhi* described in this account is a tiger shark rather than the more violent great white shark. Large tigers are known to be quite calm and can be handled relatively easily. In fact, thirty years ago in Honolulu, an enterprising fisherman took advantage of the docility of tigers and opened a "sharkquarium," called Marineland, at Kewalo Basin.

Here, a curious public paid to see young men riding on the backs of large tiger sharks. This apparently was a grand tradition of Oʻahu. In 1870, Kamakau reported that men on Oʻahu were famous for catching sharks by hand. In 1876, he colorfully reported (with an interesting analogy to the imported saddles used by contemporary *paniolo*): "To the native son, the shark was a horse to be bridled, its fins serving as the pommel of a Mexican saddle. I have seen men skilled in herding sharks riding a shark like a horse, turning the shark to this side and that until carried to shore where the shark died" (as quoted in Buck, 1964, p. 289).

Although the "sharkquarium" is gone, the exhibit tanks remain and are now used by the University of Hawaii to house bottlenose porpoises for

Above: *The Elgin Kalaniopuʻu cloak of red and yellow feathers.*

Left: *The Kiwalaʻō cape of red and yellow feathers.*

39

research in cetacean communication. To be accurate, I must add that Marineland also featured, for almost two days, a captive great white shark. To my knowledge this was the first great white shark ever to be on public display. Despite subsequent efforts by major aquariums, no great white shark has been kept alive. Like the Honolulu specimen, all have reached captivity suffering eventually fatal effects of an intense struggle during capture.

Another possible case of tiger sharks mistaken for great white sharks appears in Armine von Tempski's (1940) charming memoir of her girlhood on a large Maui ranch early in this century. She described a cattle drive from the slopes of Haleakalā to Mākena Beach. Here the cattle were pulled into the sea and dragged to a waiting ship to be hauled aboard and shipped to Honolulu. She described her father's warning about tiger sharks which appeared only infrequently but viciously attacked the floundering cattle. The infrequent occurrence and the vicious attack are far more suggestive of a great white shark.

An individual tiger shark may range over a wide area but is usually predictably and regularly present for long periods in a given area. In a study conducted at French Frigate Shoals in 1977, I and other University of Hawaii biologists tracked a large tiger shark that we had caught and tagged with a

It is very possible that the elaborate leg tattoo was associated with the strength and power of the niuhi, *the great white shark whose distinctive triangular teeth were highly valued by the ancient Hawaiians.*

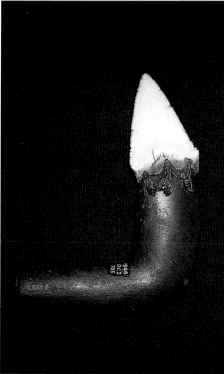

Above: *These teeth are part of a series of 21 tiger shark teeth rimming a 3-foot (90 cm) long wooden war-club. Note the careful lashing to the wood. The sennit lashing is in turn covered by what appears to be strips of whale baleen. These were probably installed to protect the lashing from being cut by teeth from another club. Several of the teeth on this war-club are broken, perhaps in a combat episode centuries ago.*

Left: *This wooden-handled knife tipped by a large great white tooth was collected on Captain James Cook's expedition to Hawai'i. It reflects the kinds of tools made by Hawaiians before Western contact. Later versions included metal blades in the same shape as the shark tooth. Ironically, metal tends to dull far sooner than the edges of a shark tooth. The tooth measures 1.5 inches wide by 1.75 inches high (3.7 cm x 4.5 cm).*

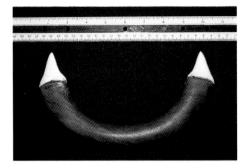

This curved fist club is tipped with great white shark teeth from a shark at least 12 feet long (366 cm). Teeth measure 1.5 inches (3.7 cm) high. A blow struck by a hand holding this weapon could create a wound as serious as that inflicted by the bite of a living shark.

sonic transmitter. Using hydrophones we could follow it by boat. Although we listened for only two days, the shark appeared to have a repeated patrol pattern around a specific area.

The story of Kapaʻaheo, the Kohala shark god, seems almost inarguably to be a great white shark. Heloke Mookini has related it to scholars at the Bishop Museum (from Bishop Museum archives):

> Long ago young girls enjoyed swimming in a lovely cove in Kohala on the Big Island. Often a swimmer would disappear and never be seen again. The people were very afraid and wanted to learn what had happened to the girls. A fisherman noticed that when a swimmer disappeared, a mysterious stranger named Kapaʻaheo could be seen sitting on the shore nearby. This fisherman then got all of the other fishermen together and they were on hand when the girls went swimming again. As before, the stranger was sitting on the rocks overlooking the cove. When he disappeared the leader of the fishermen ordered the others to dive into the water and form a protective circle around the girls. The shark swam toward the group and a huge fight began. Many

times the shark was wounded by the spears of the fishermen. Finally the shark swam away. When the men were back on shore, they found the stranger dying from many wounds that looked like they were made by fishing spears. When the man died from the wounds, he was transformed into the stone found near the edge of the cliff by the ocean.

This stone, a 9-foot (275 cm) reclining column of *pāhoehoe* lava, was moved from near the ʻUpolu Airport to Honolulu and eventually to the Bishop Museum (see p. 24). It now reclines in a lovely peaceful garden— but touch it, gaze upon its conical, pointed nose, stroke its massive length—I dare you not to hear the sharp scream of a young Hawaiian girl and see the crescent tail of a great white shark slash the ocean's surface.

Shark research can be a messy business and a source of data. Here a researcher removes two turtles and remnants of a smaller shark from the stomach of a 15-foot (458 cm) tiger shark.

Above: *Hawaiian spiny lobsters are a significant part of the diet of Hawaiian tiger sharks.*

Right: *Fledging black-footed albatross sometimes crash in the water when they are learning to fly. Before they can swim back to the landing-strip on the beach, they are devoured by tiger sharks.*

Below: *The Hawaiian monk seal is rarely seen around the high islands. The population base of this rare seal is centered in the low lying islands of the northwestern part of the chain. The waters abound with tiger sharks, its major predator.*

Hawaiian Proverbs and Sayings That Mention Sharks

'Ōlelo No'eau: Hawaiian Proverbs and Poetical Sayings
by Mary Kawena Pukui
(Honolulu: Bishop Museum Press, 1983)

'Ai a manō, 'a'ohe nānā i kumu pali
When the shark (manō) eats, he never troubles to look toward the foot of the cliff. (Said of a person who eats voraciously with no thought of who provided the food, shows no appreciation for what has been done for him, nor has a care for the morrow.)

E ao o pau po'o, pau hi'u ia manō
Be careful lest you go head and tail into the shark [manō].
(A warning to be on one's guard. Nanaue, of Waipi'o, Hawai'i, had two forms—that of a man and that of a shark. As people passed his farm to go to the beach, he would utter his warning. After they had passed, he would run to the river, change into a shark, and swim under the water to the sea where he would catch and eat those he had warned. No one knew that it was Nanaue who was eating the people until someone pulled off the shoulder covering he always wore and discovered a shark's mouth between his shoulder blades. After he was put to death the people were safe again.)

He manō holo 'āina ke ali'i
The chief is a shark [manō] that travels on land. (The chief, like a shark, is not to be tampered with.)

He niuhi 'ai holopapa o ka moku
The niuhi shark that devours all on the island. (A powerful warrior. The *niuhi* shark was dreaded because of its ferociousness. It was believed that a chief or warrior who captured this vicious denizen of the deep would acquire something of its nature.)

Ho'ahewa na niuhi ia Ka'ahupāhau
The man-eating sharks [niuhi] blamed Ka'ahupāhau. (Evildoers blame the person who safeguards the rights of others. Ka'ahupāhau was the guardian shark goddess of Pu'uloa [Pearl Harbor] who drove out or destroyed all the man-eating sharks.)

Kahu i ka lae o ka manō, he 'ale ka wahie
Kindle a fire on the forehead of a shark [manō] with waves for

fuel. (Said when food in the *imu* is not cooked because of a lack of firewood. A criticism of the hosts' half-cooked food.)

Ke one kuilima laula o 'Ewa

The sand on which there was a linking of arms on the breadth of 'Ewa. (The chiefs of Waikīkī and Waikele were brothers. The former wished to destroy the latter and laid his plot. He went fishing and caught a large *niuhi,* whose skin he stretched over a framework. Then he sent a messenger to ask his brother if he would keep a fish for him. Having gained his consent, the chief left Waīkīki, hidden with his best warriors in the "fish." Other warriors joined them along the way until there was a large army. They surrounded the residence of the chief of Waikele and linked arms to form a wall, while the Waikīkī warriors poured out of the "fish" and destroyed those of Waikele.)

Ke pau ka moa, kākā i ka nuku; ke pau ka 'iole, ahu kūkae; ke pau ka man, lanaō i ke kai

When a chicken finishes [eating] he cleans his beak; when a rat finishes, he leaves a heap of excreta; when a shark [manō] finishes, he rises to the surface of the sea. (A description of the table manners of people. Some are clean like the chicken; others are unclean, and careless, like the rat; and still others, like the shark, loll around without offering to help.)

Pua ka wiliwili nanahu ka manō; pua ka wahine u'i nanahu ke kānāwai

When the wiliwili tree blooms, the sharks [manō] bite; when a pretty woman blossoms, the law bites. (A beautiful woman attracts young men–sharks–who become fierce rivals over her. The law prevents the rivalry from getting out of hand; it can "bite." It is said that when the *wiliwili* trees are in bloom the sharks bite, because it is their mating season.)

Uliuli kai holo ka manō

Where the sea is dark, sharks [manō] swim. (Sharks are found in the deep sea. Also applied to men out seeking the society of the opposite sex.)

Wela ke kai o Ho'ohila

Warm is the sea of Ho'ohila. (Praise for a fearless warrior, or a warning that danger is near. It is said that the presence of a shark is indicated by the warmth of the sea.)

Species Accounts of Hawaiian Sharks

Like everyone else interested in sharks, I am indebted to the extensive scholarship of Leonard J. V. Compagno. The following accounts of species in Hawai'i are based, in part, on his excellent compendium *Sharks of the World*. I recommend this work to all serious students of shark biology. The two volumes include identification keys, extensive species accounts, distribution maps, and an extensive, useful bibliography.

Notes on Size

There are several ways to record the length of a dead shark, and one needs to be clear which method is being used. The two most commonly reported measures are pre-caudal length and total length. Pre-caudal length is the most straightforward measurement but excludes the tail fin and gives an underestimated impression of size. Pre-caudal length is the straight-line distance between two vertical lines: one projected from the snout, the other from the pre-caudal point. Total length can be measured at least three ways: (1) the straight-line distance between two vertical lines: one projected from the snout, the other from the tail tip held in "normal" position. This is the most natural length but can vary depending on where one decides the

Shortfin makos have shorter pectoral fins than the related longfin mako shark. Shortfins are by far the more common species in Hawaiian waters.

"normal" tail position is. (2) a calculated distance equal to the sum of the pre-caudal length and the length of the upper margin of the tail fin from the pre-caudal point to the tip of the tail. (3) the straight-line distance between a vertical projection of the snout and a vertical projection of the tail tip, taken with the shark belly down and with its tail pulled down into line with the body axis. This is the method used to make the measurements reported in this book.

Estimates of the length of live sharks are made less exactly. One biologist's rule of thumb is to record the estimated length reported by a swimmer or diver and divide by two (sharks always look bigger when they are swimming near you). A reliable way to estimate length if you are swimming with a shark is to compare it with an object when the shark swims past and later to measure that object.

Biologists rely on accurate measurements of sharks as an aid in identification. Some species that closely resemble each other can be distinguished by comparing the proportions of certain body parts, such as the length of the pectoral fin as a proportion of total length (e.g., *Carcharhinus longimanus*, the oceanic whitetip) or the length of the dorsal fin base with total length (*C. plumbeus*, the sandbar shark). I have followed the scientific convention of reporting measurements in centimeters (1 inch = 2.54 cm); total lengths are also

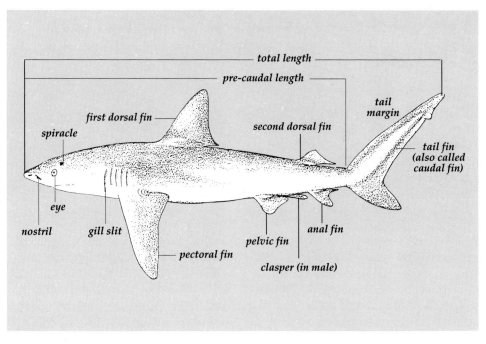

reported in feet approximated from a conversion from centimeters.

A Note to Readers who Fish and Dive

Most species of sharks have been discovered by scientists while actively studying them. However, some important finds (the megamouth shark, for example) have been accidental and have been brought to the attention of science by interested amateurs.

If you see or catch a shark that you recognize to be rare—or that you don't recognize at all—here is what to do. If you are diving, photograph the shark or look carefully at the key points. These include tail shape, relative size and placement of dorsal fins, and color of pectoral and dorsal fins and tail. Write down your observations as soon as possible.

If you catch the shark, try to salvage the specimen for scientists to inspect. Ideally, keep the whole animal iced down. Contact the Waikiki Aquarium (University of Hawaii) or the Department of Ichthyology at the Bishop Museum (both in Honolulu). Scientists will assure that the specimen is curated and studied.

Often sharks are too large to collect whole. Make measurements of at least the pre-caudal length and head length. Remove the jaws or at least a sample of teeth from both upper and lower jaws. Collect a few square inches (or centimeters) of skin from the back, sides, and belly. Take lots of photographs or video, both close-ups and wide shots. Open the stomach and record the contents so the diet of the shark can be known. Record the date, time, depth, and location where you caught your discovery.

Opposite above: *A whale shark*

Opposite below: *Galapagos sharks have large first dorsal fins, situated well forward of the free tips of the pectoral fins.*

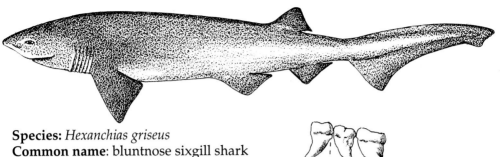

Species: *Hexanchias griseus*
Common name: bluntnose sixgill shark
Hawaiian name: unknown
Size: maximum length 482 cm (16 feet), females at 450–482 cm; size at birth 65–70 cm
Guide to identification:
This is a large shark with a broad, blunt head, a long tail, and six gill openings.
Notes on biology:
Found on the bottom to at least 1,875 m, along continental and insular shelves and upper slopes, it lives worldwide in temperate and tropical seas. In some areas bluntnose sixgills may follow prey to the surface at night. The species eats a wide variety of prey including mahimahis, small marlins, grenadiers, squids, crabs, shrimps, and is even reported to take seals.

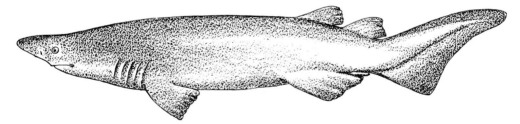

Species: *Echinorhinus cookei*
Common name: prickly shark
Hawaiian name: unknown
Size: maximum length about 400 cm (13 feet); males mature at 220 cm, females at 254 cm; size at birth less than 45 cm
Guide to identification:
There is no anal fin, the dorsal fins are set far back and are about equal in size, the tail is broad and stout, and denticles are large, separate, and star-shaped.
Notes on biology:
This is a large, sluggish bottom shark living at depths of at least 424 m on continental and insular shelves. Although the species is widespread in the western Pacific Ocean, the first specimen was discovered off the south coast of Kaua'i in 1928. It eats spurdog sharks, young bluntnose sixgill sharks, octopuses, and squids.

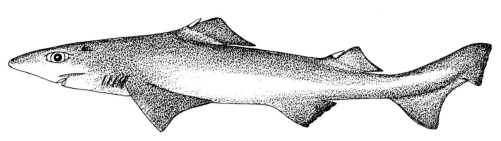

Species: *Centrophorus tessellatus*
Common name: mosaic gulper shark
Hawaiian name: unknown
Size: maximum length 89 cm (3 feet)
Guide to identification:
There is no anal fin and each dorsal fin is preceded by a short, stout spine. Rear tips of the pectoral fins are short and angular.
Notes on biology:
Found only in the western North Pacific and central Pacific Ocean, this little-known bottom shark lives at depths ranging from 260 m to 728 m. It probably feeds on fishes and squids.

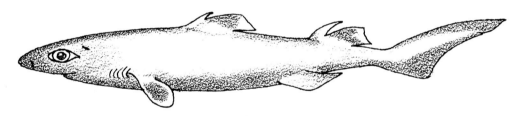

Species: *Centroscyllium nigrum*
Common name: combtooth dogfish
Hawaiian name: unknown
Size: maximum total length 50 cm
(1½ feet); males mature at 35–39 cm
Guide to identification:
This shark lacks an anal fin and has grooved dorsal fin spines. It is uniformly blackish except for white-tipped pectoral and dorsal fins.
Notes on biology:
A small, little-known deep-water shark found on or near the bottom at depths of 400–1140 m, it is also found along the western continental shelves off Mexico, central and South America, and the Galápagos Islands.

Species: *Dalatias licha*
Common name: kitefin shark
Hawaiian name: unknown
Size: to at least 159 cm (5 feet); males mature at 77–121 cm, females at 117–159 cm; size at birth about 30 cm
Guide to identification:
This is a blunt-snouted shark with equal-sized dorsal fins, no anal fin, and a stout tail. The color is grayish to blackish brown, sometimes dark violet with black spots.
Notes on biology:
Found in the warm temperate and tropical Pacific and Atlantic oceans on or near the bottom. This heavy-jawed, powerful deep-sea predator feeds on many kinds of deep-water fish as well as squids, octopuses, amphipods, shrimps, lobsters, and deep-sea worms. Kitefin sharks are reported to eat fast-swimming fish such as bonitos, perhaps by ambushing them. Off Japan, it is fished for food and the rich oil in the large liver.

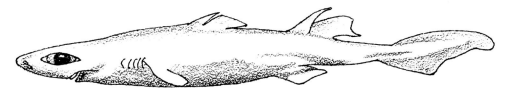

Species: *Etmopterus villosus*
Common name: Hawaiian lanternshark
Hawaiian name: unknown
Size: maximum length 46+ cm (1½ feet)
Guide to identification:
This shark lacks an anal fin and has stout dorsal finspines, the second extending beyond the top of the fin. The second dorsal fin is larger than the first. Color is dark brown or blackish on back and belly with underside of snout, mouth, and belly slightly darker. There is an indistinct black mark above the pelvic fins.
Notes on biology:
The Hawaiian lanternshark was discovered in 1905 off the south coast of Moloka‘i between 406 m and 911 m deep. The original specimen was an immature male 17 cm long. Other specimens (up to 46 cm long) have been collected, but this shark is very poorly known. Like other lanternsharks, it is named for the many tiny light-producing structures on the underside.

Species: *Euprotomicrus bispinatus*
Common name: pygmy shark
Hawaiian name: unknown
Size: maximum total length 27 cm (10 inches); males mature at 17–19 cm, females at 22–23 cm; size at birth 6–10 cm
Guide to identification:
This is a small shark with a large head, large spiracles, and small gill slits. Both dorsal fins are spineless: the first fin small, the second with a long base. All fins with conspicuous light edges. Body is blackish.
Notes on biology:
Found in deep water, 1,800–9,900 m, throughout the world's warm temperate and tropical oceans, these sharks migrate vertically daily from deep midwater to the surface and back. All known specimens have been taken at the surface at night. They eat deep-water squids and vertically migrating fishes and crustaceans. This species may be the world's smallest shark.

Species: *Isistius brasiliensis*
Common name: cookiecutter shark
Hawaiian name: unknown
Size: maximum total length about 50 cm; males mature at 31–37 cm, females mature at 38–44 cm
Guide to identification:
This is a small shark with a short snout and cigar-shaped body

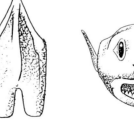

(before its feeding habits were known, this shark was called a "cigar shark"), no anal fin, small dorsal fins set far back, large spiracles on top of the head, and greatly reduced gill slits. It is brownish with a prominent darker band encircling the body over the gill regions.
Notes on biology:
This species is found throughout tropical oceans. All sharks are fascinating but the cookiecutter leads an especially intriguing life about which we know little. Although small, the cookiecutter preys on large fish and marine mammals such as yellowfin tunas, mahimahis, swordfishes, porpoises, elephant seals, megamouth sharks, and in one reported case, the rubber covering of an instrument attached to a nuclear submarine. In Hawai'i in 1992, the body of a drowning victim

recovered off Wai'anae, O'ahu, bore several cookiecutter wounds (see case 97 in Register of Shark Attacks). No one has ever seen a cookiecutter in the act of biting, but there is good circumstantial evidence for its predatory habits. A biologist working in Hawai'i (Jones, 1971) noted the cookie-sized holes in tunas for sale in the fish market. He inspected teeth and stomach contents of cookiecutter specimens. Using "cookiecutters" made from the teeth and jaws of *Isistius* specimens, he was able to duplicate the scars in fish flesh. This species certainly seems to have some of the expected adaptations for such predatory habits but bafflingly lacks others. The upper teeth are needlelike, probably to pierce and attach to the prey's muscle mass. The lower teeth are broadly triangular and interlocked at their bases. Biologists assume that the cookiecutter shark rotates its body during a bite and the lower band of teeth cuts the plug of flesh. As the picture on the previous page shows, the jaws are protrusible, and the cookiecutter has what scientists call "suctorial lips." How much time a bite requires is not known. The large spiracles permit respiration while the mouth is involved in prolonged feeding. Biologists have many questions about the behavior of cookiecutters. Chief among them is: how does this small shark with greatly reduced fins manage to approach its large, fast-swimming prey? Cookiecutters have very large, oily livers, which may reduce their density in seawater. The resulting relative lightness may aid their swimming and tenacity. The entire lower surface of the body trunk is covered with bioluminescent organs. Freshly caught specimens glow a ghostly green. Perhaps the cookiecutter attracts prey with its green glow and then ambushes the would-be predator, turning the dinner-tables on it. Like the related pygmy sharks, cookiecutters migrate vertically from deep midwater to near the surface. Specimens have been caught in trawls over a wide depth range, from the surface to 359 m.

Above: *This adult study specimen of a cookiecutter shark is near the maximum size of the species. Though small, cookiecutter sharks regularly take bites out of tunas, mahimahis, porpoises, and swordfishes.*

Right: *In the lower row, the triangular teeth of the cookiecutter shark overlap one another at their bases to form a strong cutting edge that resembles a band-saw blade. Teeth in the upper jaw are much narrower and needlelike. Note the large nostrils at the tip of the snout and the loose, flexible lips, which probably aid in feeding.*

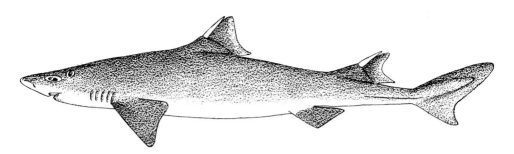

Species: *Squalus asper*
Common name: roughskin spurdog
Hawaiian name: unknown
Size: maximum length 118 cm (4 feet); males mature at 85–90 cm, females at 89–118 cm; size at birth 25–28 cm
Guide to identification:
There are large spines before both dorsal fins, almost exceeding the height of the dorsal fin; a broad rounded snout; no anal fin; lateral keels at the base of the tail. Color is dark gray or brown on back and sides, lighter on chest and belly. Dorsal, pectoral, and tail fins lack obvious white edges.
Notes on biology:
This species is found on or near the bottom on continental and insular shelves including the Gulf of Mexico and South Africa at depths of 214–600 m. It eats squids and fishes.

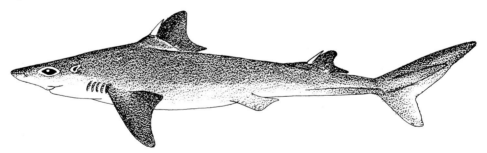

Species: *Squalus mitsukurii*
Common name: shortspine spurdog
Hawaiian name: unknown
Size: maximum length 110 cm (3½ feet); males mature at 65–89 cm, females at 72 cm; size at birth is about 22–26 cm
Guide to identification:
This species has long spines before both dorsal fins (but relatively shorter than those in *S. asper*, not extending the full length of the fin margin), no anal fin, and a lateral keel at the base of the tail.
Notes on biology:
This shark is widespread in the world's warm oceans, on or near the bottom at depths of 165–518 m. It eats fishes, shrimps, squids, and octopuses.

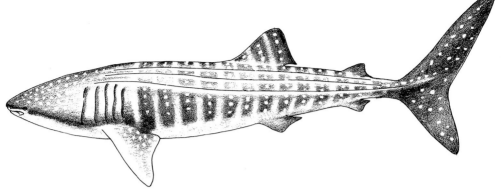

Species: *Rhincodon typus*
Common name: whale shark
Hawaiian name: perhaps *lele wa'a*
Size: maximum length uncertain, possibly to 1,800 cm (59 feet), certainly to 1,200 cm (40 feet); females at 438–562 cm; smallest juveniles found are less than 50 cm. This species is considered to be the world's largest fish.

Guide to identification:
The huge size and wide, flattened head are sufficient to identify the whale shark. However, free-swimming specimens less than 100 cm long have been taken alive in the central Pacific. The whale shark's mouth extends the full width of its head. Body color ranges from blackish blue to brownish rust with a distinctive pattern of light spots and horizontal and vertical stripes. Three to four longitudinal ridges, sometimes quite pronounced, extend along the upper body on each side from head to tail. There are pronounced keels at the base of the tail.

Notes on biology:
Whale sharks are found throughout the tropical oceans of the world. They are fairly commonly seen by sportfishermen, boaters, and small-plane pilots off the lee shores of O'ahu and Hawai'i. They are apparently migratory and wide ranging, occurring in the open sea and coastal waters. Whale sharks also enter the lagoons of coral atolls (Taylor and Nolan, 1978). Whale sharks are one of three plankton-feeding species of sharks (see basking shark and megamouth shark). They feed on a wide variety of organisms from masses of small shrimps to anchovies, mackerels, small tunas, and squids. Whale sharks encountered by divers and swimmers are quite docile and allow humans to hitch rides on their backs. Despite their large size, whale sharks do well in aquariums with very large tanks. Twenty-foot-long specimens are popular attractions at the Ring of Fire Aquarium in Osaka, Japan, and the

This front-on view of a juvenile whale shark shows the fact that the mouth encompasses the entire width of the head. Note the extremely tiny teeth, relatively large tongue, and the scrolled nostrils connected to the mouth.

Although whale sharks are widely recognized as the world's largest fish, juvenile whale sharks can be quite small. This specimen was taken alive in the central Pacific by tuna purse seiners. It still bore the vitelline scar revealing the connection site of the tube that linked the developing shark to the nutrition of the egg yolk.

Okinawa Expo Aquarium. Biologists are not certain about the mode of reproduction in this species but believe it to be oviparity (i.e., egg-laying).

Only one whale shark egg case has ever been reported. The shape and size of a rugby football, it was dredged up from 250 feet from the bottom of the Gulf of Mexico. More than six juvenile specimens are preserved in scientific collections. All are less than 100 cm long and all bear a vitelline scar (commonly and incorrectly called a shark belly button) between their pectoral fins. This scar disappears in adults but represents the attachment point of the pseudo-umbilicus that connected the young to the yolk sac in the egg. All of these small free-swimming specimens were found in the central Pacific not near the surface but in water thousands of feet deep. They were collected by commercial tuna fishermen who lacked the facilities to keep the juveniles alive, so they were frozen and donated to scientific collections. The fact that these juveniles were found in such deep water so far from shore suggests that perhaps the reproductive mode is what biologists term ovoviviparous. The female retains the egg case inside her body and the young shark hatches from the egg case inside the mother. She then gives birth to the recently hatched shark. Thus, the egg case found in the Gulf of Mexico might have been prematurely released by a mother.

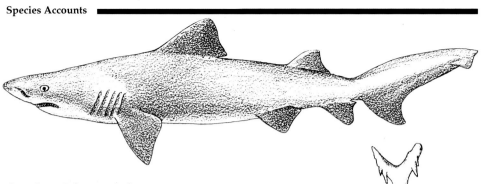

Species: *Odontaspis ferox*
Common name: smalltooth sand tiger
Hawaiian name: unknown
Size: maximum length 360 cm (12 feet); males mature at 275 cm, females at 300+ cm; size at birth 105 cm
Guide to identification:
This is a large, bulky shark with a conical snout; the mouth is long and extends to a point past the eye. Color is medium gray; young individuals have black-tipped dorsal fins.
Notes on biology:
Smalltooth sand tigers are inhabitants of deeper waters in tropical and warm temperate seas including the Pacific, Atlantic, and Indian Oceans and the Mediterranean Sea. There are few records from Hawai'i. They eat fishes, squids, and shrimps. The related sand tiger shark, *Eugomphodus taurus*, looks somewhat similar and is commonly displayed in large aquariums in the mainland United States and Europe.

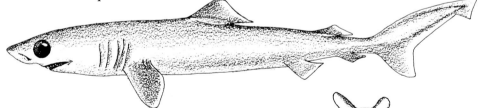

Species: *Pseudocarchariias kamoharai*
Common name: crocodile shark
Hawaiian name: unknown
Size: maximum total length 110 cm
(3¹/₂ feet); males mature at 74–110 cm, females at 89–102 cm; size at birth about 41 cm
Guide to identification:
This is a small shark with very large eyes, long gill slits, and the first dorsal fin set well back.
Notes on biology:
This is the smallest member of the group that includes makos, great whites, megamouths, sand tigers, and other "lamnoids." The crocodile shark occurs well

offshore in tropical waters around the world ranging from the surface to at least 300 m. Its large eyes suggest that it may be active at night. The jaws are quite protrusible. The teeth are long and slender and resemble those of the related mako sharks. Little is known about what it eats.

Species: *Megachasma pelagios*
Common name: megamouth shark
Hawaiian name: unknown
Size: maximum known length of males 515 cm
Guide to identification:
The head is large and the greatly distensible mouth has a silvery lining. The body is blackish brown on the back and sides, with creamy undersides. The bottoms of the pectoral fins are whitish with black leading edges; the tops are blackish brown with white tips and trailing edges. The tail is large and fleshy. Special elongated structures (covered with flattened denticles) filter shrimps and other prey from food-filled water taken into the mouth. The thick muscular tongue probably forces the filtered water out the gill openings and rinses the food off the filtration structures into the stomach. The structure of the tiny needlelike teeth (as well as other internal features) are thought to indicate relationships with other lamnoid sharks such as makos and the great whites.

Notes on biology:
Megamouth I, the first megamouth known to science, was accidentally caught off northeastern Oʻahu on 15 November 1976 by a crew of researchers aboard a research launch from Kāneʻohe Bay. A retrieved nylon drogue used to station the boat in deep water was entangled with a 446-cm-long unknown shark. The researchers salvaged the barely dead specimen and contacted me at the University of Hawaii's Waikiki Aquarium. After a baffling preliminary look, I concluded

Megamouth I, shown here, like all subsequently collected megamouths, had a very silvery lining to its large mouth. It has not yet been confirmed whether this mouth lining also contains photophores capable of producing light to attract tiny shrimps in the dark water where megamouths feed.

When Megamouth I was captured off northeastern O'ahu in 1976, U.S. Navy researchers brought it to dockside in Kane'ohe Bay. In lifting the animal the tail was pulled off. Although this carcass looks limp and ugly, it was an extremely beautiful sight to me. No biologist had ever seen a representative of this novel family of sharks. With the help of colleagues, I was fortunate to acknowledge this discovery.

that not only was this a new species of shark but it was distinctive enough to warrant naming a new genus and new family. This discovery was reported extensively in the popular press, but the formal scientific description was not published until 1983. The type specimen was deposited in the research collection of the Department of Ichthyology at the Bishop Museum in Honolulu. Subsequently, five more specimens have been identified from accidental catches at various locations. All have been mature males. No females or juveniles have been reported. Megamouth II (449 cm long) was caught in a gill net off Catalina Island, California, in November 1984. This preserved study specimen is on display at the Los Angeles Museum of Natural History in California. Megamouth III (515 cm long) was stranded ashore near Perth, Western Australia, in August 1988. The specimen is preserved at the Western Australian Museum. Megamouth IV (approximately 400 cm long) was caught near southern Japan, but only photographs were taken; no specimen or samples were kept. Megamouth V (490 cm long) was caught in June 198° near the same area as Megamouth IV and released alive. Megamouth VI (494 cm long) was caught in a gill net off Dana Point, California, in October 1990. After study and photography, it was released alive.

Megachasma pelagios (based on the Greek words for "giant yawner of the open sea") is one of three known species of plankton-feeding sharks. The other two species (the temperate-water basking shark, *Cetorhinus maximus*, and the tropical whale shark, *Rhincodon typus*) feed fairly close to the sea surface, but megamouth sharks evidently often feed in deeper water. Judging from the stomach contents of specimens of megamouth sharks, this species feeds on the pelagic community called the "deep scattering layer" (DSL). The DSL was discovered during research on sonar and sound transmission in the sea after World War II. Depth sounders work by transmitting sound pulses toward the bottom and timing the return of the echo that bounces back from the dense sea floor: the deeper the water, the longer the return time. Researchers noticed that very often they would receive a false bottom signal—a deep layer of something that scattered their sound signals. Interestingly, the depth of the DSL varied over a 24-hour period: deeper during the day, shallower at night. The darker the night (e.g., no moon, rain), the shallower the DSL, sometimes coming almost to the sea surface. Early explanations for the DSL suggested it was caused by sound-affecting density differences due to salinity or temperature. Very soon investigators confirmed that the sound signals were bouncing off the tiny bodies of fishes, shrimps, salps, and other planktonic forms. As biologists increasingly studied the DSL, they found it throughout the world's oceans. The species that composed the layered community varied from area to area but it was basically composed of similar species. Most DSL species migrate vertically to maintain station at low light levels. Major constituents of the DSL and of the stomach contents of megamouth specimens are euphausiid shrimps, many species of which are bioluminescent. They are small, about the size of a nail paring. Until Megamouth VI was collected, all information about the species was obtained from dead specimens.

The fishermen and biologists who collected the sixth known example of this interesting species towed it to the harbor at Dana Point, California, and tied it to a dock with a long rope lashed to its tail. Diving photographers and scientists were able to photograph and swim closely around it, stroking it, and learning about the living shark. After 24 hours, they towed it back to sea. Before releasing the still-active shark, scientists attached a battery-powered sonic transmitter to its back, near the dorsal fins. Megamouth VI was tracked for almost 48 hours by using hydrophones. The sonic tag sent back regular signals revealing the shark's depth and location. The shark went deeper in daylight hours and shallower at night, preliminary evidence that it might have been following the DSL. The Megamouth VI episode suggests they are hardy animals that can survive capture. We could learn much about their biology from similar studies. There is certainly much to know. Here are two of the many questions yet to be answered:

All sharks have some ability to protrude their upper jaw. It is highly protrusible in megamouths. The dark band at the base of the lower jaw normally fits right in front of the eyes when the mouth is closed. In this study specimen, Megamouth I, the mouth has been distended for demonstration.

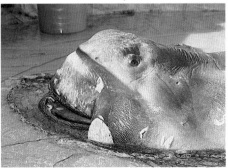

(1) Where are the females?

Several of the captured males had turgid, fluid-filled claspers, indicating that they might have been captured close to a sexual encounter.

(2) Do megamouth sharks have a bioluminescent mouth?

Biologists have speculated that megamouths may attract or concentrate prey animals by emitting a silvery light from the inside of its mouth. This hypothesis is based on two observations: the euphausiid shrimps found in the stomachs of megamouths are known to produce biological light, and the very silvery oral lining of the mouth is studded with what appear to be specialized pores. The tissue in Megamouth I was too deteriorated to provide evidence, and histological work on Megamouth II was inconclusive.

Megamouths I–VI were found or captured accidentally. It is likely that the discovery and subsequent captures are related to increased use of gill nets in offshore commercial fisheries. We need to make a concerted effort to find and study more living specimens. This could probably be accomplished by monitoring the DSL in an area where megamouths have been collected (such as around Oʻahu or off Southern California) and setting specially rigged gill nets within the DSL community. Remote-operated video cameras and lights could be trained on the net. Captured sharks could be saddled with battery-powered instrument packages such as sonic transmitters that send continuous information about depth, light level, and temperature. After tagging, the sharks could be released and monitored.

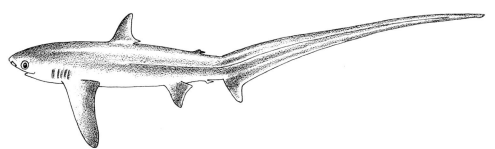

Species: *Alopias pelagicus*
Common name: pelagic thresher
Hawaiian name: perhaps *manō ʻula* or *laukāhiʻu*
Size: maximum total length 330 cm (11 feet); males mature at 276 cm, females at 264–300 cm; size at birth about 96 cm (Remember that these are total lengths; the very long tail is almost equal to the pre-caudal length.)
Guide to identification:
The head is strongly arched between the eyes with an elongated snout and nearly straight forehead. The back and sides are grayish blue. This is the smallest of the three species of thresher sharks.
Notes on biology:
This oceanic species is widespread in the Indo-Pacific region, from eastern Africa and the Red Sea to Mexico and the Galápagos Islands. Primarily a pelagic species, this thresher is sometimes caught near shore. It ranges in depth from the surface to at least 150 m. These threshers are caught by the long-line fishery off Hawaiʻi.

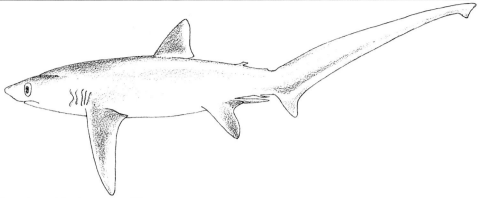

Species: *Alopias superciliosus*
Common name: bigeye thresher
Hawaiian name: perhaps *manō 'ula* or *laukāhi'u*
Size: maximum length about 461 cm (15 feet); males mature at 270 cm, females at 335+ cm; size at birth 106 cm (Remember that these are total lengths; the very long tail is almost equal to the pre-caudal length.)

Guide to identification:
As its name indicates, the large eyes are diagnostic, their upper margins extending onto the top of the head, which is nearly flat. There is a deep horizontal groove on the nape on each side above the gills.

Notes on biology:
These threshers are a significant element in the long-line catch around Hawai'i. This is a wide-ranging species found in coastal waters over continental shelves around the world and in open tropical seas. Specimens have been caught as deep as 500 m. Biologists would like to know much more about the feeding habits of threshers, but believe that they stun small prey fishes by striking them with their large tail.

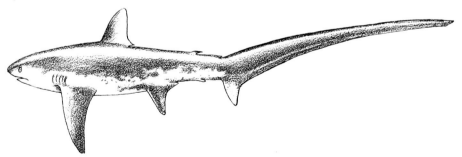

Species: *Alopias vulpinus*
Common name: thresher shark
Hawaiian name: perhaps *manō 'ula* or *laukāhi'u*
Size: maximum total length 549+ cm (18 feet); males mature at 320+ cm, females at 376+ cm; size at birth 114–150 cm (Remember that these are total lengths; the very long tail is almost equal to the pre-caudal length.)

Guide to identification:
The head is strongly arched between the eyes, but the snout is shorter than in the

pelagic thresher. The pectoral fins are rounded, and the white color of the belly extends above the pectoral bases. Much of the literature on Hawaiian sharks has confused this species with *A. pelagicus*.

Notes on biology:
These sharks are an element of the Hawai'i long-line catch. Off Southern California they are fished with commercial gill nets. Megamouth II was accidentally caught in such a fishing operation. This may be the most common and widespread of the three species of threshers. It is found around the world in warm seas.

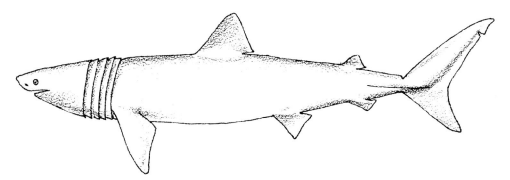

Species: *Cetorhinus maximus*
Common name: basking shark
Hawaiian name: unknown
Size: maximum length 900 cm (29 feet)—although there are unconfirmed reports of larger specimens); males mature at 400–500 cm, females at 810 cm; size at birth unknown

Guide to identification:
These are large sharks with enormous gill slits that almost encircle the head, a pointed snout, and a crescent-shaped tail. The skin is brownish, with sharp hooked denticles that point forward, backward, and sideways. This is one of three species of plankton-feeding sharks (see also whale shark and megamouth shark).

Notes on biology:
This species is normally found in temperate waters of the continental shelves of the Americas, East Asia, Australia, Europe, and South Africa, where they filter-feed on plankton in near-surface waters. Only one specimen has been reported from Hawai'i. In June 1983, a 28-foot specimen was stranded on a remote beach at Pilale Bay on the Hāna coast. Biologists from the Waikiki Aquarium and the National Marine Fisheries Service identified the shark as *Cetorhinus maximus* and collected samples of teeth and skin for deposit at Bishop Museum. Vagrant animals from temperate continental waters are unusual in Hawai'i but do occur. For example, in 1978, George Balazs of the National Marine Fisheries Service observed a live northern elephant seal hauled up on the beach at Midway. A female, she bore a metal tag affixed at San Miguel Island off California by researchers from the University of California at Santa Cruz. Also, the rare presence of great white sharks in Hawai'i (far more common in California and Oregon) may be examples of animals crossing to Hawai'i from the eastern Pacific.

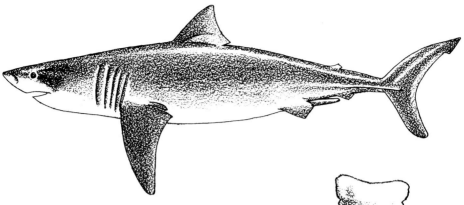

Species: *Carcharodon carcharias*
Common name: great white shark
Hawaiian name: *niuhi*
Size: maximum length probably about 640 cm (21 feet) although unsubstantiated reports of specimens over 800 cm (26 feet) have been published; males begin maturing at about 240 cm; size at birth probably at least 125 cm

Guide to identification:

Great white sharks are easily recognized by the combination of pointed snout; high gill slits; powerful, deep body; almost symmetrical crescent-shaped tail with strong lateral keels at the base; and distinct (but often irregular) margin above the white belly and trunk on the lower third of the sides. Color is dark bluish or blackish gray with a marked (but often irregular) margin above the white belly and trunk on the lower third of the sides. Teeth are distinctly triangular with serrated margins. The related makos share many of the external characteristics mentioned above but have very differently shaped teeth.

The pointed, conical snout of the great white shark is diagnostic of the species. This photograph is unusual because it documents an unblemished great white shark. Most photographs show the bruised and bloodied noses damaged by the shark's crashing into baited shark cages used by many photographers.

Notes on biology:

Great white shark teeth were used in Hawaiian tools and weapons collected on the expeditions of Captain Cook. Since 1874 there have been nine substantiated records in the Hawaiian Islands, including a live captive specimen and at least two attacks, one fatal (e.g., see cases number 5, 17 and 50 in the Register of Shark Attacks). There were convincing reports of sightings off Kaho'olawe and Maui in 1990 and 1991. All records are of adults. In areas where they are more common (e.g., California, southern Australia), great white sharks are known to be significant predators of seals and sea lions. Perhaps long ago in

PHOTO BY MARTY SNYDERMAN

65

Hawai'i, when there were more monk seals around the Islands, there were also more great white sharks. It has been suggested that great white sharks might trail the migrating humpback whales from the Pacific Northwest to Hawai'i when the whales make their annual winter visit for courtship and reproduction. Although fatal shark attacks on humans in Hawai'i are probably due to large tiger sharks, one should always consider the possibility that the attacking shark could be a great white.

Species: *Isurus oxyrinchus*
Common name: shortfin mako
Hawaiian name: unknown
Size: maximum length about 394 cm (13 feet); males mature at 195 cm, females at 280 cm; size at birth 60–70 cm
Guide to identification:
Earlier works on Hawaiian sharks called this species *Isurus glaucus*. The streamlined makos have spindle-shaped bodies, conical snouts, and long daggerlike teeth. The tail is crescent shaped, with strong keels along the tail base. The "shortfin" refers to the fact that the pectoral fin is shorter than the head (i.e., from the tip of the snout to the last gill slit). In contrast, the "longfin" mako has a pectoral fin that is longer than the head.

Notes on biology:
Shortfin makos have been called the peregrine falcons of the shark world. They are very fast, and active, and are prodigious jumpers. They are esteemed by anglers as one of the most challenging of all big fish to catch on hook and line. Shortfins are found over a wide area of the world's oceans, from the Aleutians to Tierra del Fuego and West Africa to East Africa, around the world.

Species: *Isurus paucus*
Common name: longfin mako
Hawaiian name: unknown
Size: maximum length about 417 cm (14 feet); males mature at 245 cm, females at 245 cm; size at birth 97 cm
Guide to identification:
The longfin mako has relatively longer pectoral fins than the closely related shortfin mako. It is also more slender, has a blunter snout, and straighter center teeth.
Notes on biology:
Biologists know far less about this rarer mako. Longfins are found throughout the tropical oceans, usually well offshore. They are not common in Hawai'i.

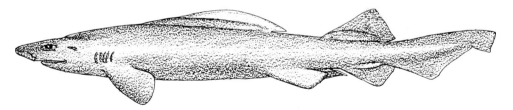

Species: *Pseudotriakis microdon*
(formerly called *P. acrages* in the reports of Tester and other Hawai'i researchers)
Common name: false cat shark
Hawaiian name: unknown
Size: maximum length about 295 cm (10 feet); males mature at 200–269 cm, females at 212+ cm; size at birth 70–85 cm
Guide to identification:
This large, bulky dark-brown, deep-water shark can be recognized by the combination of elongated feline eyes; large lateral spiracles, wide mouth extending

behind the eye; low, long-based first dorsal fin; high second dorsal fin set far back; and its relatively small tail.

Notes on biology:
Little is known about its diet, but the small, sharp teeth and very large mouth suggest that this shark may gulp fairly large fishes and invertebrates on the deep bottoms (200–1,500 m) where it dwells. False cat sharks are also found in coastal Asia, East and West Africa, the western North Atlantic, Europe, and the British Isles.

Shark control and fishing programs in Hawaii have also collected rarely seen Hawaiian sharks such as this false cat shark. Note the extremely large spiracles behind each eye and the muscular but flaccid body.

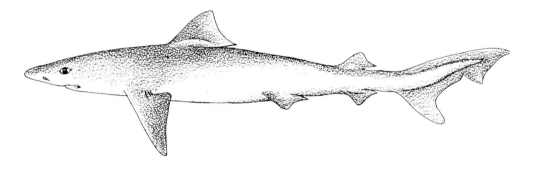

Species: *Galeorhinus galeus*
Common name: tope shark
Hawaiian name: unknown
Size: maximum length 195 cm (6½ feet); males mature at 120–170 cm, females at 130–185 cm; size at birth 30–40 cm

Guide to identification:
This slender, long-nosed houndshark has large, oval eyes. The first dorsal fin is relatively large; the second dorsal is small, about equal in size to the anal fin.

Notes on biology:
Tope sharks are fairly common along continental shelves in the temperate waters of the west coast of North and South America, Europe, West Africa, and South Australia. They prey on a wide variety of fishes and are the subject of important commercial fisheries for their excellent flesh. There is only one record of this shark in Hawai'i, from Laysan Island.

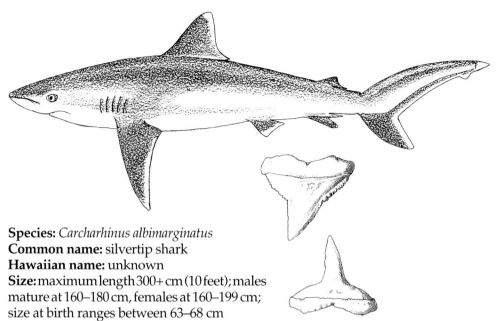

Species: *Carcharhinus albimarginatus*
Common name: silvertip shark
Hawaiian name: unknown
Size: maximum length 300+ cm (10 feet); males mature at 160–180 cm, females at 160–199 cm; size at birth ranges between 63–68 cm

Guide to identification:
Silvertips are fairly large and slender, with distinctive white tips and margins on all fins. The pectoral fins are narrow and pointed; the first dorsal is narrowly rounded.

Notes on biology:
This species is widespread in the Indo-Pacific, occurring from coastal East Africa to the Gulf of Panama. It is abundant adjacent to insular shelves and offshore banks from the surface to 600–800 m.

Silvertips patrol steep coral drop-offs well away from the reef and seem to swim just on the far edge of a diver's vision. Although their behavior has not been well studied, observers have noted that silvertips are confident but not aggressive when encountered by divers. They eat a variety of reef and offshore fishes and seem to dominate other reef sharks around boats. Given their predilection for islands and their wide distribution in the tropical western and eastern Pacific, it seems unusual that no silvertips are reported from Hawai'i. I include them here in the hope that divers and other ocean enthusiasts will take careful note and report any sightings of this species. Sharkwatchers should be especially alert for silvertips around the buoys moored offshore (Fish Aggregating Devices [FADs]) and in deep areas visited by tourist submarines.

The silvertip shark is widely distributed and represented in just about every tropical island group in the Pacific Ocean. Strangely, it has not yet been recorded from Hawai'i.

PHOTO BY FOSTER BAM

69

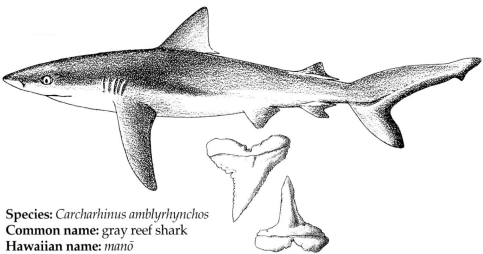

Species: *Carcharhinus altimus*
Common name: bignose shark
Hawaiian name: *manō*
Size: maximum length about 300 cm
(10 feet); males mature at 216–267 cm,
females at 226–282 cm; size at birth 70–90 cm

Guide to identification:
Bignose sharks have a long, bluntly rounded snout; long pectoral fins; a relatively
high first dorsal fin; and lack distinctive markings on the uniformly gray body and
fins.

Notes on biology:
Although reported from Hawai'i, this is not a common shark within the archipelago.
It is common on the continental shelves of warm temperate and tropical North and
South America, West Africa, the Red Sea, and the Indian Ocean. Bignose sharks are
caught commercially in the Caribbean region. They feed on fishes, sharks, and
stingrays near the bottom in depths of 90–430 m.

Species: *Carcharhinus amblyrhynchos*
Common name: gray reef shark
Hawaiian name: *manō*
Size: maximum length 233–255 cm (8 feet), but most specimens are about 160 cm (5
feet); males mature at 130–145 cm, females at 122–137 cm; size at birth 45–60 cm

Guide to identification:
These are medium-sized gray sharks with a broadly rounded snout, round eyes, and distinctive black margins on the tail, second dorsal fin, and anal fin.

Notes on biology:
Gray reef sharks are the hallmark shark of Indo-Pacific tropical islands. Their range extends from Madagascar through Indonesia and northern Australia to Hawai'i. Gray reef sharks are active, strong swimmers and apparently social. They form daytime packs in some areas, notably the reef passes connecting the open ocean to the inner lagoons. At one such place in the Tuamotu Islands (Rangiroa Atoll), their aggressive posturing was first filmed by Al Giddings and Dewey Bergman. This pioneering work was followed by the research of Donald Nelson and Richard Johnson (in Tahiti and Enewetak Atoll) who described what is apparently a threat display of the species. When approached too closely or when startled by quick movements, a threatened gray reef shark points its pectoral fins downward, arches its back, and swims in an exaggerated manner. The shark wags its head and tail and may even sometimes swim in a spiral. As discussed elsewhere in this book, adult female gray reef sharks aggregate seasonally over shallow reef areas in Hawai'i, a behavior apparently now limited to the unpopulated northwestern Hawaiian Islands. It is probable that hundreds of years ago, such aggregations were common among the high islands and may have been directly related to the ancient Hawaiian 'aumakua beliefs.

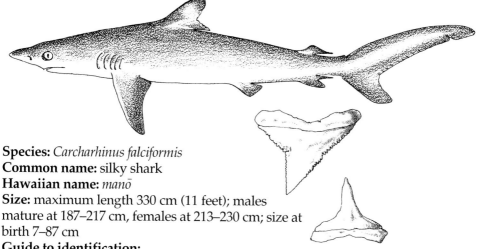

Species: *Carcharhinus falciformis*
Common name: silky shark
Hawaiian name: *manō*
Size: maximum length 330 cm (11 feet); males mature at 187–217 cm, females at 213–230 cm; size at birth 7–87 cm

Guide to identification:
These are large, dark, slim oceanic sharks with relatively short pectoral fins.

Notes on biology:
Silky sharks are found throughout the world's tropics from East Africa through the Pacific, the Caribbean, and West Africa. They are abundant offshore and sometimes are found far from land in the open sea. They may occur in waters as shallow as 15 m and in the open ocean from the surface down to at least 500 m. They are primarily fisheaters, dining on a variety of species from tunas to porcupine fishes but also squids and pelagic crabs. Silkies are often associated with schools of tunas and are viewed as a nuisance by tuna purse seiners because of the net damage they cause.

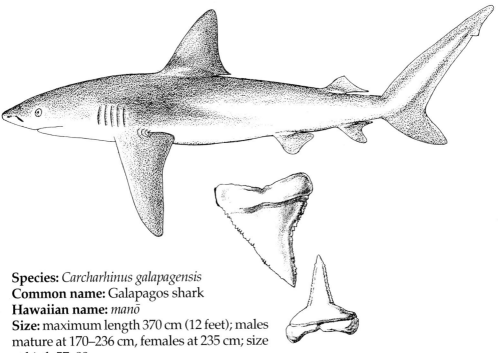

Species: *Carcharhinus galapagensis*
Common name: Galapagos shark
Hawaiian name: *manō*
Size: maximum length 370 cm (12 feet); males mature at 170–236 cm, females at 235 cm; size at birth 57–80 cm

Guide to identification:

Galapagos sharks are large, gray animals with a moderately rounded snout and a high dorsal fin with its origin behind the point of the pectoral attachment. Individuals vary in coloration but often have dusky trailing edges to their tail fins.

Notes on biology:

Although named for the island group where it was discovered by Stanford scientists in 1905, *C. galapagensis* is widely distributed in tropical oceans. This is probably the most abundant nearshore shark in the northwestern Hawaiian Islands and may have been much more common around the high islands 200 years ago. I have swum in groups of more than two dozen Galapagos sharks around Laysan Island. They are curious but not aggressive in the Hawaiian Islands, but have been implicated in attacks on humans elsewhere. They have also been seen to swim in a conspicuous posture similar to that described for gray reef sharks. Galapagos sharks feed primarily on bottom fishes including eels and triggerfishes.

The Galapagos shark, despite its insular name, is a fairly common shark in Hawai'i, particularly in the northwestern Hawaiian Islands.

PHOTO BY MARTY SNYDERMAN

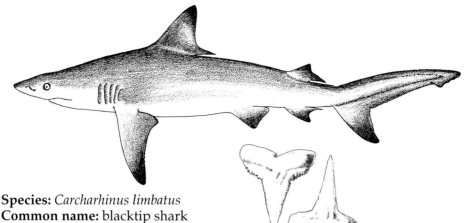

Species: *Carcharhinus limbatus*
Common name: blacktip shark
Hawaiian name: perhaps *manō pā'ele*
Size: maximum size 255 cm (8¹/₂ feet); males
mature at 135–180 cm, females at 120–190 cm; size at birth 38–72 cm
Guide to identification:
The blacktip shark is a very different species from the blacktip reef shark, *C. melanopterus*. Blacktip sharks are large and fairly stout, with a long, pointed snout. The black tips of the fins are not distinctly demarcated and the tail fin usually lacks a black margin.
Notes on biology:
Blacktip sharks are found through the tropical and subtropical oceans, both inshore and offshore, but are not truly oceanic. In continental areas, they commonly occur off river mouths and in shallow muddy bays. In Hawai'i, they are not common but have been seen by viewers on tourist submarines off O'ahu. Blacktips are primarily fish eaters but also eat octopuses, squids, crabs, and lobsters as well as juvenile sharks.

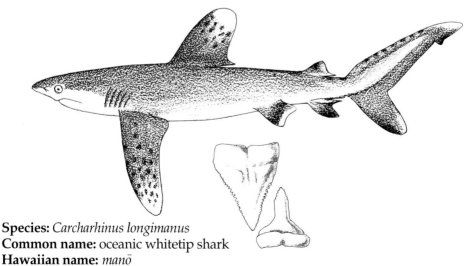

Species: *Carcharhinus longimanus*
Common name: oceanic whitetip shark
Hawaiian name: *manō*
Size: maximum length 350–395 cm (13 feet) but most are under 300 cm (10 feet); males

mature at 175–198 cm, females at 180–200 cm; size at birth 60–65 cm

Guide to identification:
Oceanic whitetips can be easily distinguished by their elongated pectoral fins, high rounded first dorsal fin, and the white tips on the pectorals and first dorsal. Despite the similar common name, this species is very distinct from the whitetip reef shark, *Triaenodon obesus*.

Notes on biology:
These oceanic sharks are found throughout the world's tropical and

The scientific name of the oceanic whitetip, C. longimanus, seems well chosen when one considers its large pectoral fins.

warm temperate waters. In the Hawaiian Islands, they are found well offshore. They are occasionally seen around Fish Aggregating Devices (FADs are large buoys moored in deep water off the high Hawaiian Islands to assist commercial and sportfishing). Oceanic whitetip sharks have been implicated in human attacks.

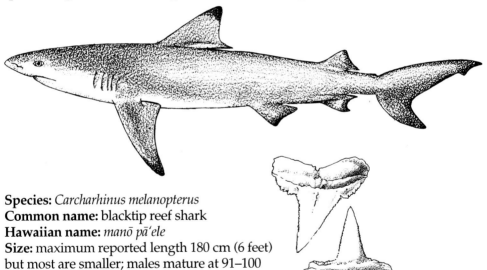

Species: *Carcharhinus melanopterus*
Common name: blacktip reef shark
Hawaiian name: *manō pāʻele*
Size: maximum reported length 180 cm (6 feet) but most are smaller; males mature at 91–100 cm, females at 96–112 cm; size at birth 33–52 cm

Guide to identification:
The distinctive, sharply demarcated blackfin tips make this graceful shark easy to distinguish. The body color of juveniles found over light-colored sand bottoms in tropical Pacific lagoons tends to be tan. Adults patrolling deeper reef waters have gray bodies with white undersides.

Notes on biology:
Blacktip reef sharks have apparently entered the eastern Mediterranean through the Suez Canal from the Red Sea, but they are most common in the Indian Ocean, the Indo-Australian region, and the central Pacific. Young blacktip reef sharks were once commonly found in shallow lagoons (like the sandbars of outer Kāneʻohe Bay) and

shallow reef flats (eastern Lāna'i). In Pacific atoll lagoons they are fairly abundant and are known to nip the ankles and calves of waders. It is possible that shark bites occasionally suffered in Hawai'i by windsurfers and boardsurfers who suddenly fall off their boards into shallow water are the work of disturbed blacktip reef sharks. These beautiful sharks, when very young, are perfectly proportioned scale models of much larger sharks. This makes them very attractive to large public aquariums. They are easily caught and shipped, and they thrive in aquariums.

Species: *Carcharhinus plumbeus*
Common name: sandbar shark
Hawaiian name: *manō*
Size: maximum reported length 239 cm (7 feet) but most are smaller; males mature at 131–178 cm, females at 144–183 cm; size at birth 56–75 cm

Guide to identification:
Sandbar sharks are easily distinguished by the extremely tall, triangular first dorsal fin with its origin over the pectoral base. Earlier writers (including Tester) called this species *C. milberti.*

Notes on biology:
Sandbar sharks are abundant in temperate tropical waters of the Atlantic, Pacific, and Indian oceans. Sandbars were the most commonly caught species in A. L. Tester's Hawaiian research programs in the 1960s. This species supported a large fishery in the Gulf of Mexico area. Richard Wass (1971, 1973) at the University of Hawaii studied the Hawaiian population and compared it with Atlantic counterparts. No clear migrating pattern has yet been seen in Hawai'i. Along the eastern seaboard of the United States, however, sandbar sharks migrate annually, heading south for warmer waters in the winter and north in summer. Sandbar sharks feed on a variety of reef fishes and are preyed upon by tiger sharks and great white sharks. So far, this species has not been associated with any human attack. Sandbar sharks do well in large public aquariums, growing to 8–9 feet long. Occasionally, small specimens can be seen swimming in the excellent displays at the Waikiki Aquarium and Sea Life Park.

Species: *Galeocerdo cuvier*
Common name: tiger shark
Hawaiian name: *niuhi*
Size: maximum reported length 550 cm (18 feet); males mature at 226–290 cm, females at 250–350 cm; size at birth 51–76 cm

Guide to identification:

Tiger sharks are almost unmistakable. Distinctive characteristics include blunt head with straight margin, small pectoral fins, and tigerlike markings. These are more obvious in juveniles and can be difficult to see in adults. Body color ranges from brownish to bluish gray, with darker stripes overlaying the basic color. Tooth shape is unique.

Young Brothers (founders of the inter-island freight company) often took paying customers offshore to fish for sharks, using dead Honolulu wagon horses for bait.

PHOTO PROVIDED BY BISHOP MUSEUM

Notes on biology:

The tiger shark's diet is comprised of various slow-swimming fishes (e.g., puffers), octopuses, crabs, sharks, rays, porpoises, seabirds, turtles, lobsters, garbage, and an array of other items. Because meals like turtles and lobsters take longer to digest than soft-bodied fishes, it is difficult to measure from stomach contents the relative abundance of food types eaten by an individual shark. Tiger sharks are believed to periodically evert their stomachs, in order to get rid of indigestible matter (such as turtle scutes) too large to defecate. Records of the stomach contents of tigers likely over-represent the dietary importance of turtles because the indigestible shell parts may be retained for weeks without being regurgitated. In contrast, soft-bodied prey (e.g., fishes, octopuses) are quickly digested and leave little or no signs of their presence. Tiger sharks are found throughout the world's tropics. These are probably the most dangerous sharks in tropical waters. Although they are big and dangerous, they can tire quickly and become fairly docile.

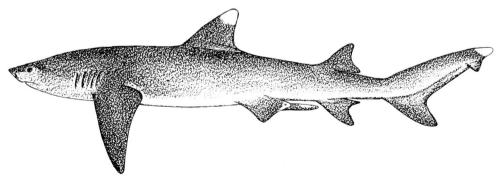

Species: *Prionace glauca*
Common name: blue shark
Hawaiian name: unknown
Size: maximum length 385 cm (12½ feet), but there are unsubstantiated reports of larger specimens; males mature at 182–281 cm, females at 221–323 cm; size at birth 35–44 cm

Guide to identification:
The most obvious characteristic of this beautiful open-ocean shark is its deep blue body color with white below. Blue sharks are slender and graceful and have long pectoral fins. Blues are widespread in the world's oceans. They feed on spawning squids in the submarine canyons of Monterey Bay, eat krill in the southern Pacific Ocean, and catch flying fish offshore of Hawai'i.

Notes on biology:
This species is wide-ranging and migrating, traveling in partial response to water temperature and food supply. Sharks tagged off Virginia have been recovered off Spain. See Strasburg (1958) for an older but excellent study of the distribution of blue sharks in the central Pacific Ocean.

Species: *Triaenodon obesus*
Common name: whitetip reef shark
Hawaiian name: *lālākea*
Size: maximum length 160 cm (5 feet), but there are unsubstantiated reports of

larger specimens; males mature at 105 cm, females at 105–109 cm; size at birth 52–60 cm

Guide to identification:
Whitetip reef sharks are easy to distinguish. The combination of distinct white fin tips; short, broad snout; oval eyes; and rear-positioned first dorsal fin are distinctive. Compagno has described the combination of down-slanted mouth and prominent brow ridges as "giving its face a sardonic, disgusted look."

Notes on biology:
Whitetip reef sharks are probably the most popular sharks in Hawai'i. They are fairly common, easily approached, phlegmatic, and non-aggressive. Divers even feed them fish and squid by hand. Their natural diet includes reef fishes, eels, lobsters, and crabs. Individuals return to the same cave for long periods. They are believed to maintain home ranges of up to several square kilometers. See Randall's (1977) excellent study of their natural history.

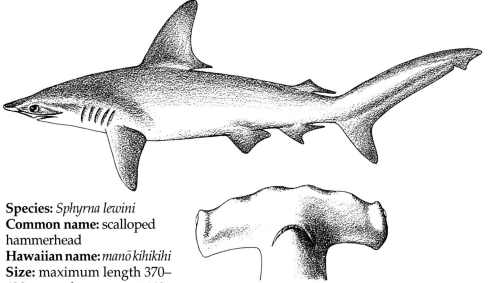

Species: *Sphyrna lewini*
Common name: scalloped hammerhead
Hawaiian name: *manō kihikihi*
Size: maximum length 370–420 cm; males mature at 140–165 cm, females at about 212 cm; size at birth 42–55 cm

Guide to identification:
The head is broad (between the eyes) and narrow (from front to back). When viewed from below or above, the front margin of the head is scalloped, with an indentation at the midline (compared with *S. zygaena*, which has almost a smooth margin with only slight scalloping and no median indentation). Mouth size is relatively small compared with that of other shark species of similar size. Color tends to be gray-brown on the back and sides, and white on the lower sides and undersurface, with dusky or black-tipped pectoral fins.

Notes on biology:
These may be the most abundant sharks in the world's warm oceans, occurring along the tropical coasts of all continents. In Hawai'i, pups are born in spring in shallow embayments like Kāne'ohe Bay, Honolulu Harbor, and Pearl Harbor. As the sharks

grow, they move into increasingly deeper water. Fishermen commonly catch juveniles on hooks and in nets. Biologists at the University of Hawaii have learned much about the Oʻahu populations. In 1971, Dr. Thomas Clarke (see Bibliography) published an important study of hammerheads conducted on specimens caught in gill nets in and around Kāneʻohe Bay. In 1991, Dr. Kim Holland and his graduate students at Hawaii Institute of Marine Biology began studies using sonic tags to track the movements of free-living hammerheads. Schooling of adults has been studied in the Gulf of California, Mexico, by Klimley and others (1981) but has not been reported in Hawaiʻi.

There are several unsubstantiated explanations for the unique shape of the head in this family of sharks. Perhaps it acts as a diving plane, or forward wing (called a canard in aircraft design), that increases swimming efficiency and maneuverability. Perhaps the broad head serves to spread out sensory fields of the Lorenzini ampullae. The wide head may also help in trapping prey against the bottom. The wide separation of the paired nostrils, in which are located complexes of nerve endings (nasal rosettes), could aid in pinpointing a source of attractive odors. Scalloped hammerheads eat a wide variety of fishes and invertebrates including eels, halfbeaks, lizardfishes, jacks, goatfishes, damselfishes, wrasses, butterfly fishes, surgeonfishes, blacktip reef sharks, squids, octopuses, mantis shrimps, crabs, and lobsters.

These three hammerheads show clearly the reason for the name "scalloped hammerhead."

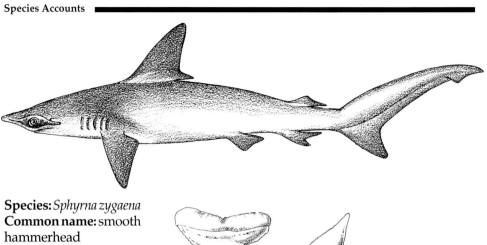

Species: *Sphyrna zygaena*
Common name: smooth hammerhead
Hawaiian name: *manō kihikihi*
Size: maximum length 370–400 cm; adults mature at about 210–240 cm; size at birth 50–61 cm

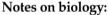

Guide to identification:
Smooth hammerheads have a broad, narrow-bladed head with an almost smooth front edge (compared with that of the scalloped hammerhead). They are dark olive or dark gray brown above and white beneath, and the underside of the pectoral fin tips is dusky.

Notes on biology:

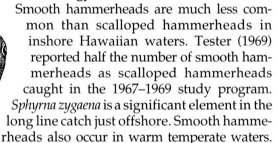

Smooth hammerheads are much less common than scalloped hammerheads in inshore Hawaiian waters. Tester (1969) reported half the number of smooth hammerheads as scalloped hammerheads caught in the 1967–1969 study program. *Sphyrna zygaena* is a significant element in the long line catch just offshore. Smooth hammerheads also occur in warm temperate waters. They are recorded from Northern California and the eastern North Atlantic. This species feeds on a variety of fishes and invertebrates, including mackerels, small sharks, stingrays, shrimps, and squids.

Isurus oxyrinchus (shortfin mako)
Perhaps the most prized sportfish by some anglers is the shortfin mako, famous for its high-speed swimming and acrobatic jumping. In Michael Cole's painting, we see a shortfin mako about to bite down on the squid lure favored by the trolling sportfishers of the Kona coast. Like their relatives, the great white sharks, makos have strong crescent-shaped tails with lateral keels and massive muscles to strengthen and drive the tail.

Another important adaptation for high-speed swimming in makos is their ability to raise their body temperature above that of the ambient water. This gives added swimming efficiency to their muscles and a slight edge over their prey. Their large gill slits, also a characteristic shared with the related great white sharks, permit efficient respiration during high-speed swimming.

Shark Watching in Hawai'i

There is a thrilling fascination in watching a predator move—the speed of a hunting cheetah, the stretch of a sated lion, the towering hulk of a grizzly bear. In the sea, the thrill has the added dimension of unfamiliar surroundings. Whether it is the seal-swallowing killer whale or the turtle-devouring tiger shark, the predators of the sea make our heart beat faster when we encounter them.

With any predator we have an intellectual interest. But the thrill comes from the emotions—the innate fear that we could be the prey, we could die in the jaws of the beast.

Sharks, especially large sharks, inspire such thrills and fears. The enormous popular fascination harnessed by *Jaws*, the book and the movie, confirms the phenomenon. Although our basic dread might be innately based on survival, as the chapter on shark attacks shows, there are perfectly rational reasons to be careful around sharks, too.

Yet most of us are attracted to sharks.

Sphyrna lewini (Scalloped hammerhead)
In early April, adult female scalloped hammerheads leave the deeper waters off the reefs of the high islands and enter shallow bays like Pearl Harbor, Kāne'ohe Bay, Honolulu Harbor, and Hanalei Bay. Here they give birth to their litters of 15–31 pups, each about 12 inches long. After pupping, the females return to their deeper-water haunts, leaving their young progeny to fend for themselves. As the young hammerheads grow larger, they gradually move closer to the mouths of the bays and eventually take up residence in the same area from which their mothers came.

We want to watch them, to admire them, to enjoy their grace and power—if we can do so safely. Of course, one person's safety is another person's danger. Adventuresome tourists in South Australia pay thousands of dollars to dive (in the safety of an aluminum shark cage) with great white sharks, sometimes accompanied by Rodney Fox, a survivor of a near-fatal shark attack by a great white.

In Tahiti, local entrepreneurs schedule daily dives with gray reef sharks. At each shark-watching session, spectators in scuba gear stay behind a rope stretched across and above the bottom, like a balcony railing at the ballet. Tour leaders use fresh fish to lure the star attractions, usually gray reef sharks, to a safe distance in front of the audience.

In Hawai'i, divemasters hand-feed friendly whitetip reef sharks as regular demonstrations for diving tourists. Molokini Islet, near Wailea, Maui, is an especially popular location for this activity.

In my opinion, it is far better to observe the natural behavior of wild animals with as little disturbance as possible. I saw my first tropical shark in the wild—a 3-foot gray reef shark—in 1963 at Johnston Island, southwest of Hawai'i. The University of Hawaii had sent me and some other graduate students to collect reef fishes and eels for research. At the end of the first day of work dives, my neck was strangely stiff. My more experienced diving partners explained that the sore muscles were due to the constant swiveling of my head, as I continuously looked for the inevitable shark.

On the third day, when I finally saw the fearfully sought-for animal, my nervousness strangely and immediately left. The shark expressed some passing interest in my presence, then went about her business. Once the shark had swum into my view, the overwhelming urge was not to flee but to watch this graceful, wonderful creature. I talked to many other divers about this abrupt change in attitude and it seems to be a common response. (However, I have never compared notes with anyone whose first view of a shark was a 15-foot great white swimming straight for them.)

This turn-of-the-century group proudly posed with their shark catch after a day's outing.

PHOTO PROVIDED BY BISHOP MUSEUM

All fear can be dispensed with if one chooses the safest places for shark watching—on dry land or on the deck of a boat. In turn-of-the-century Hawai'i, when tourism was young, shark fishing was one of the exciting pastimes offered to visitors. Two brothers named Young (whose name lives on in the company they founded) had a city contract to dispose of the carcasses of horses that had died in the service of hauling wagons, carriages, and trolleys around Honolulu. The easiest resting place for horses for the Young Brothers to reach was offshore of southwestern O'ahu.

When the carcasses were dumped overboard, sharks often came around. Rather than waste such an opportunity, the operators invited paying customers to come along and watch the action as sharks fed on horses and fishermen harpooned and shot tiger sharks. After landing the "tigers of the deep," as one author wrote, "Souvenirs were in order…teeth were extracted and cuts of skin sliced off, rough as a horseshoer's rasp" (Scott, 1968).

There is still plenty of shark fishing in Hawai'i today but dead horses are no longer featured. Deep-sea sportfishermen occasionally hook mako sharks, which are recognized as gamefish by the International Gamefishing Association. In spring and summer, anglers fishing from docks in Honolulu Harbor and Kāne'ohe Bay frequently catch juvenile scalloped hammerheads. The catches of commercial fishing boats are on view most mornings at the wholesale fish markets in Honolulu and Hilo. Various species of sharks are accidental catches on the long-line boats that fish mainly for mahimahi, 'ahi, and billfishes.

For many years, commercially caught shark meat was processed into kamaboko (Japanese fish cake) but

Walking the huge shark are Marineland employes Francis Warren, left, and Gordon Kaeolio. —Star-Bulletin Photo

The large outdoor pools of the commercial Honolulu Marineland featured displays of young men riding large Hawaiian tiger sharks. In March 1961, the operators landed a 13-foot great white shark off the mouth of Honolulu Harbor. It lasted only two days before it died but it was seen by many visitors. This was the first semisuccessful attempt to keep great white sharks in captivity. These tanks are now used by the University of Hawaii Marine Mammal Laboratory.

public acceptance of shark steaks and filets was low. In the 1970s, the State of Hawaii and the Sea Grant Office at the University of Hawaii promoted the marketing of fresh shark so that the incidental (but significant) catch of shark would not be wasted. The program was successful, and fresh shark meat is frequently seen in supermarkets and restaurants.

Foreign vessels fishing offshore with long lines catch many sharks, including threshers, oceanic whitetips, and occasionally blue sharks. The drying dorsal, pectoral, and tail fins of the catch can be seen festooning the rigging of these boats as they provision in Honolulu and Ala Wai Harbor.

In 1991 and 1992, several shark attacks (two fatal; see chapter on Shark Attacks) stimulated fishing programs to remove dangerous tiger sharks from nearshore areas. Crowds of onlookers came to see the catches of several 13–15-foot-long sharks, and newspapers featured front-page photos.

In earlier days, before the growing population of Hawai'i filled coastal waters with powerboats, freighters, and intense commercial fishing, one could probably see sharks swimming near beaches and reefs. In the unpopulated, protected northwestern Hawaiian Islands (e.g., Lisianski, Laysan, Pearl and Hermes Reef) large sharks frequently swim in the shallows. Today, in the main islands, there are still a few places where one can see sharks from the shore: the reefs of Lāna'i, sandbars in Kāne'ohe Bay, and some reefs off north Kona and Kohala.

The most reliable and safest places (for both humans and sharks) to watch sharks in Hawai'i are on O'ahu. Sea Life Park, near Waimānalo, is one of the few aquariums in the world that successfully displays scalloped hammerheads. The large reef tank also hosts blacktip reef and whitetip reef sharks and, sometimes, gray reef sharks. Staff members

This juvenile Hawaiian whitetip reef shark is being carefully packed in oxygenated seawater within an insulated box for air shipment to a mainland public aquarium. There it will grow into an adult. Perhaps it will mate and bear the next generation as sharks from Waikiki Aquarium have done at Sea World parks in San Diego and Florida. Shipping sharks when they are young assures survival, economical air freight, and the opportunity for millions of aquarium visitors to see sharks thrive and grow in public aquarium displays.

of Sea Life Park have also doubled as shark fishermen after local attacks.

In Honolulu's Kapi'olani Park, the Waikiki Aquarium (a department of the University of Hawaii) has a fine display of living Hawaiian sharks as well as educational programs, museum exhibits, and a theater, all featuring information about shark biology and their importance in Hawaiian culture.

Staff members of this aquarium have long been involved in research on sharks. Their accomplishments include the discovery and naming of the Megamouth, research on the biology of tiger sharks, and the pioneering work of collecting and transporting live blacktip reef sharks to aquariums around the world. The aquarium also serves as an information center for shark research and current activities

PHOTO BY TOM KELLY

86

and events involving sharks.

Allied to the Waikiki Aquarium is the Hawaii Institute of Marine Biology at Coconut Island in Kāne'ohe Bay. This research complex is not generally open to the public, but occasional tours are sometimes scheduled. The large outdoor shark ponds have long been used by University of Hawaii researchers and often host sharks (including oceanic whitetips) waiting to join their fellows on display at the Waikiki Aquarium. Small sharks are also displayed in outdoor ponds at the Mauna Lani Bay Hotel in south Kohala, island of Hawai'i.

For guaranteed satisfaction in shark watching—safe and dry—visit Sea Life Park and the Waikiki Aquarium. But be careful when you cross the street after you leave—roadways are statistically far more dangerous than tropical waters.

Above: *Before the coastal waters of the high Hawaiian Islands were the site of intensive recreational and commercial boating activity, it is likely that large sharks approached the shore closely. This Galapagos shark swims close to the beach in the unpopulated waters of French Frigate Shoals, part of the northwestern Hawaiian Islands.*

Below: *The author, in the lower left of the picture, swims across the shallow reef flat off Laysan to observe a crowd of milling female gray reef sharks.*

87

Shark Attacks in Hawai'i

George H. Balazs, National Marine Fisheries Service, Honolulu Laboratory

(Note by Leighton Taylor: I am particularly grateful that George Balazs has allowed me to include his excellent and exhaustive case by case compilation of shark attacks in Hawai'i. George has combined scholarship with his humane, ethical, and friendly personality both to search archives and to interview victims and their families. By doing so he has assembled a reliable and useful compendium of information about human relationships with sharks in Hawai'i.)

Shark interactions with humans have at least three possible causes. The differences among them need to be considered when reviewing these records. Some attacks (few in proportion to the total) are motivated by feeding behavior. Tiger sharks eat a wide variety of animals and especially tend to strike floating objects. Occasionally they mistake a human swimmer or surfer for their normal prey. Great white sharks eat seals, sea

---

Carcharodon carcharias (great white shark)
This speculative view shows a great white shark about to be hooked by a Hawaiian fisherman. The painting is based on several items of indirect evidence. Certainly Hawaiians made good use of great white sharks, as evidenced by tools and weapons collected on Captain Cook's visits to Hawai'i.

The ancient Hawaiians also crafted large fishhooks (called kīholo). From carved pieces of wood, the hooks were tipped with strong, sharpened bone. Whale bone was favored. A curved shape was formed by lashing branches of a living tree and then harvesting the wood after it had grown into acceptable shape, or an entire hook might be carved from whale bone.

lions, porpoises, and other mammals. They make mistakes too.

Many sharks are opportunistic eaters and will salvage meals from animals dead from other causes. Usually the source of these meals is a dead marine animal—a whale carcass, perhaps. Sometimes the source of these meals is a drowned human.

The most probable cause of a shark attacking a human is behavioral and not hunger. Many inshore sharks appear to be territorial, at least about their personal space if not an actual area of the reef (although this is possible too). When a shark is threatened, it reacts aggressively, sometimes by striking a warning posture, sometimes by suddenly biting the intruder. Such behavior is similar to that of a watchdog biting a mail carrier. The dog is not trying to eat the delivery person; neither is the shark trying to eat the swimmer or diver.

Of course, there is another circumstance in which people are injured by sharks. When a person hand-feeds a shark or interferes with its natural behavior by pulling its tail, spearing it, or some other form of molestation, biting can result. This is called "asking for it," and we warn against it.

The following list, current through December 1992, has appeared in several earlier publications starting in 1981 (see Balazs and Kam 1981, 1983; Balazs 1987, 1992). Prior to 1981 there were no comprehensive lists for shark attacks in the Hawaiian Islands.

The list includes 101 cases spanning the period 1779 through 1992. Forty-four (43.6%) of the 101 cases are tabulated as having involved a fatality. However, nine of the 44 fatalities (20.5%) are considered to have been likely due to drowning or other causes, which was then followed by shark bite or dismemberment. No cases have been included on this list in which a person was known with certainty to have been dead prior to being bitten by a shark.

Cases of shark attack presented in this list all involve some form of physical injury to the person resulting from a shark. Cases in which "only" the person's equipment was attacked (bitten) are not included. Nevertheless, several cases of this nature have occurred in Hawaii that are of significance. They will be compiled into a separate list at a later date. For example, in October of 1990 Greg Filtzer was lying on his 9-foot long surfboard in Hanalei Bay on Kaua'i when a 12-foot shark bit the board and violently pulled

Joe Thompson was body boarding off northern Kaua'i in October 1985 (case no. 75) when a tiger shark approached him head-on, bit through the board, and severed Joe's right hand.

it and Greg backwards underwater. In the process the shark completely removed a 14-inch wide half-moon shaped piece from the surfboard. Without so much as a scratch, Greg miraculously reached shore safely after the shark released the board. Greg's brother-in-law was on a surfboard next to him and witnessed the entire event.

Below left: *Sea turtle with severed flipper, another casualty of hungry sharks.*

Below right: *This survivor bears the healed crescent-shaped scar of a large shark bite. (The seal's head is to the right of the photo and the hind flippers to the left.)*

Shark Attacks by Activity

Activity	Fatal	Nonfatal	Total
Swimming/snorkeling	8	15	23
Spearfishing while snorkeling	1	5	6
Scuba diving	3	1	4
Spearfishing while scuba diving	2	0	2
Hard-hat diving	0	1	1
Surfboarding	2	13	15
Body ("boogie") boarding	2	3	5
Sail boarding	0	1	1
Body surfing	1	2	3
Surfing on an air mattress	1	0	1
Floating on an inner tube (with lobsters)	0	1	1
Wading	0	1	1
Fell into sea from shore or swept out to sea	16	0	16
Fell off boat or boat capsized	3	1	4
Net fishing	0	3	3
Crabbing	1	2	3
Removing shark from fishing line/gaff	0	3	3
Dynamite fishing	1	0	1
Fishing (type unknown)	2	1	3
Activity unknown	1	4	5
Total	**44**	**57**	**101**

Source: George H. Balazs, National Marine Fisheries Service, Honolulu Laboratory

Shark Attacks in the Hawaiian Islands by Species of Shark

Shark species	Fatal cases	Nonfatal cases	Total
Tiger shark	3	4	7
Great white shark	1	1	2
Hammerhead shark	0	2	2
Cookiecutter shark	1	0	1
Subtotal	5	7	12
Unknown species, large	20	9	29
Unknown species, small	1	8	9
Unknown species, unknown size	18	33	51
Subtotal	39	50	89
Total	**44**	**57**	**101**

Source: George H. Balazs, National Marine Fisheries Service, Honolulu Laboratory

Shark Attacks in the Hawaiian Islands Involving Fatalities

a = Death directly due to shark attack.
b = Death likely due to shark attack.
c = Death likely due to drowning or other trauma following shark attack.
d = Insufficient information on which to base an opinion as to cause of death.

Years	(a)	(b)	(c)	(d)	Overall Fatal	Overall Nonfatal	Total
1990–present	2	3	2		7	7	14
1980–1989		2	3	4	9	15	24
1970–1979			1	2	4	8	12
1960–1969			1	3	3	5	8
1950–1959	3		1	3	7	7	14
1940–1949				1	1	5	6
1930–1939				1	1	5	6
1920–1929	1				1	2	3
1910–1919		1		1	2	1	3
1900–1909	2		1	3	6	2	8
1779–1899	2			1	3	0	3
Total	10/44	6/44	9/44	19/44	44	57	101
	22.7%	13.6%	20.5%	43.2%			

Source: George H. Balazs, National Marine Fisheries Service, Honolulu Laboratory

Shark Attacks in the Hawaiian Islands by Month for the Years 1879–1992

Month	Fatal	Nonfatal	Total
January	3	2	5
February	2	5	7
March	2	4	6
April	7	9	16
May	2	1	3
June	3	6	9
July	4	2	6
August	4	3	7
September	2	5	7
October	1	6	7
November	4	4	8
December	3	5	8

Note: Data are for the 89 cases in which the month of attack is known. Cases occurred during the month of April every year for the six-year period of 1986–1991.

Source: George H. Balazs, National Marine Fisheries Service, Honolulu Laboratory

Register of Shark Attacks in the Hawaiian Islands, 1779–1992

KEY

COMPILER'S OPINION AS TO CAUSE OF FATALITY

* Fatality involved

[a] Fatality *directly* attributed to shark attack.

[b] Fatality *likely* attributed to shark attack.

[c] Fatality *likely* attributed to another cause (drowning, etc.) besides shark attack which was followed by mutilation or dismemberment by shark or sharks.

[d] *Insufficient information upon which to base an opinion as to cause of death*, although mutilation and/or dismemberment by sharks had occurred. Fatality may have been directly attributed to shark attack, or may have resulted from another cause. This category also includes an absence of any witnesses or the absence of sufficient body remains to determine cause of death by autopsy.

SOURCE: The following table was compiled by George H. Balazs, National Marine Fisheries Service, Honolulu Laboratory. Complete documentation for each case accompanies copies of this table deposited in the Pacific Collection in Hamilton Library, University of Hawaii, and at the Southwest Fisheries Science Center, Honolulu Laboratory of the National Marine Fisheries Service, 2570 Dole Street, Honolulu, Hl 96822–2396.

Case no.	Date	Location	Victim
1*a	1779	Maliu, Hawai'i	Nu'u-anu-pa'a hu
2*a	1828	Lahaina, Maui	Male
3*d	2 June 1886	Hāmākua, Hawai'i	Two females
4*c	14 July 1900	Makapu'u Point, O'ahu	Emil Uhlbrecht and an unidentified person
5	Early 1900s	Inter-Island Dry Dock at Kaka'ako Street, Honolulu, O'ahu	Emil A. Berndt
6*a	8 Aug. 1902	Kalihi, O'ahu	Young male
7*d	1904	Honolulu, O'ahu	Male
8*d	1907	Pepe'ekeo, Honomū Hawai'i	Male
9	8 Oct. 1907	Kalepolepo, Kīhei, Maui	Male
10*a	17 Jan. 1908	Mānā, Kaua'i	Male
11*d	10 Apr. 1909	Pa'uwela, Maui	Mrs. Ah Kim Chong

Young male gashed on one side of buttocks after being pursued while surfboarding. Subsequently suffered "great pain" and died at Pololū.

"A man out riding surf at 'Uo was killed by a shark which bit off his limbs and left his body floating." Attack witnessed by a number of Hawaiian chiefs.

Washed into the sea while fishing from shore; one woman found bitten (fatal), the other woman disappeared.

Believed to have drowned when carried out to sea while hunting seashells with companions. "A thorough search was made for the body for several days." Victim's foot with skin and flesh intact "in a fair state of preservation" was found in the stomach of an 11-ft, 9-in shark hooked on the night of 17 Aug. 1900 off Kaka'ako, Honolulu, by John Kinipeki. Positive identification of victim made by Mrs. Uhlbrecht, based on an ingrown toe nail. Human pelvis and femur, blackened and totally denuded of flesh, were also recovered from the shark's stomach. These bones were thought to be from a different person, probably one of several Chinese fishermen lost overboard in the harbor during past months.

Young boy severely chafed when a large shark swam between his legs.

Pulled under while crabbing; both arms amputated.

Partial remains of swimmer who had disappeared two days earlier off Diamond Head found in the stomach of a "monstrous shark." Body was complete from the waist down with the exception of one leg. Shark also contained ducks, tin cans, and wood.

Bitten while fishing.

Arm amputated at the elbow while retrieving fish caught in net.

Pulled under while gathering fish stunned by dynamite.

Nineteen-year-old woman reported to have been swept away by waves while gathering 'opihi along the rocky shoreline. Search party saw a large shark devour what appeared to be part of the missing woman's body.

Case no.	Date	Location	Victim
12	Apr. 1910	Pearl Harbor, O'ahu	Martin Lund
13*d	1910	Hilo, Hawai'i	Male
14*b	3 Mar. 1914	Honomū, Hawai'i	Okomoto
15	28 Sept. 1922	Keawanui, Kamalō, Moloka'i	Male
16	7 Apr. 1926	Hilo Bay, Hawai'i	Mrs. Leonard Carlsmith
17*a	18 May 1926	Hale'iwa, O'ahu	William J. Goins
18	13 June 1931	Pearl Harbor, O'ahu	Lieutenant Williamson
19*d	2 Sept. 1931	Kāhala, O'ahu	George Gaspar
20	16 Feb. 1932	Lahaina, Maui	Male
21	4(?) Sept. 1936	Lahaina, Maui	Young male

Unprovoked attack on a hard-hat diver. Authenticity questioned by Baldridge.

Bitten while fishing.

Washed into the sea while picking *'opihi* and attacked by two large sharks.

Bitten while inspecting wharf.

Severely bitten while swimming 25 yards from shore near the Hilo Yacht Club at 5:30 P.M. "The shark with one bite terribly lacerated her right leg from the heel to the thigh. The calf of her leg was torn nearly to shreds, and the part of her limb above the knee was laid open to the bone." A long necktie was applied as a tourniquet to her leg as soon as she was brought to shore. "Anesthetics" were required twice at the hospital to treat the wounds. According to the victim, the shark that bit her "had a mouth about three feet wide."

Gave a sudden shriek, then disappeared while swimming at Hale'iwa; remains of body found in 12.5-ft great white shark caught off Kahuku.

End of one of the victim's fingers amputated while using a gaff to bring a 10-ft tiger shark aboard a boat after harpooning it. Shark also bit in half the 2-in oak pole of the gaff. The following items were found in the shark's stomach: hind leg of a mule, two bathing suits nearly digested, soldier's belt buckle, a pint of buttons, two horseshoes, corner of a wooden soapbox, anchor chain, two small anchors, and assorted bolts, nails, and copper fittings.

Swept out to sea by strong currents while fishing; remains of body found in 18-ft shark caught off Barbers Point.

Sailor from U.S. Navy vessel *Saratoga* bitten while swimming about 1 mile off Māla Wharf. Two wounds each 6 inches long were inflicted.

Leg "badly cut" requiring 19 stitches at the Lahaina Hospital. Swimming with several other children near the "old wharf" when a shark was sighted. Victim disappeared under water for a few seconds, then came to the surface and "made a frantic effort for land." "A large shark was seen again the following morning."

Case no.	Date	Location	Victim
22	30 Dec. 1936	Honokōhau, Maui	John Kekuhi
23	4 Oct. 1939	Kāne'ohe Bay, Mōkapu, O'ahu	James Akina
24	1 July 1941	Nānākuli, O'ahu	Hisao Shimoto
25*d	5 Apr. 1943	McGregor Point, Maui	Leonard Gant
26	1943	Midway, northwestern Hawaiian Islands	Male
27	1943	Midway, northwestern Hawaiian Islands	Male
28	27 June 1947	Mākaha, O'ahu	Valentine Limatoc
29	19 Sept. 1948	Makapu'u, O'ahu	Noah Kalama
30*c	16 Jan. 1950	Kahakuloa, Maui	Gilbert S. Hotta

Bitten on the thigh while diving underwater trying to retrieve the body of a drowning victim wedged between two rocks. Three deep gashes sustained that required hospitalization. Shark reported to be 20 ft.

Bitten on hand by 5-ft shark while spearfishing in shallow water.

Bitten on arm while removing 100-lb shark from fishing line.

Disappeared while swimming with three companions after the small boat they were canoeing swamped in high seas. Swamping occurred 3 miles from shore. Victim vanished shortly before reaching land after he fell behind the other swimmers. On 29 Apr. 1943, the "decomposed remains" of the victim's "right forearm" and "brightly colored swimming trunks" were "found in the stomach of a 16-ft shark" caught in turtle nets set out at night "near the Koa house" by Kihei fisherman Alex Akina. Shark's stomach also contained a piece of newspaper dated 25 Mar. 1943. Note: this case was erroneously reported by Gilbert (1963) and Baldridge (1974) as "Leonard Gaut, 4/15/53, O'ahu."

Unprovoked attack, but unable to determine circumstances.

Unprovoked attack, but unable to determine circumstances.

Bitten while spearfishing with six other men.

Bitten on leg while swimming.

Swept into the sea with two companions by a large sudden wave while fishing at night from the rocky base of an overhanging cliff. Another companion (Wayman Fujimoto) managed to cling to the rocks when the wave hit. The partial remains of Gilbert Hotta were recovered from a "huge shark" caught on the morning of 19 Jan. 1950 by rescue workers searching the immediate area. The "badly battered remains" of one of the other missing fishermen (Harold Fujimoto) was also recovered floating nearby. The body of the third fisherman (Hideo Tamura) was never found.

Case no.	Date	Location	Victim
31*d	25 June 1951	Kapehu Beach, Laupāhoehoe, Hawai'i	Alejandro Nodura
32*d	3 Aug. 1952	Ala Moana, O'ahu	Shigeichi Kawamura
33*a	3 Dec. 1952	Maile, O'ahu	Gerbacio Solano
34	18 Feb. 1953	Barbers Point, O'ahu	James S. Takeuchi
35	4 July 1953	Ka'ula Rock	David Crick
36*a	26 July 1953	Maile, O'ahu	Harold Souza
37	2 Sept. 1953	Waiau, Pearl Harbor, O'ahu	Daniel Gonsalves
38*d	8 Apr. 1954	Wailupe, O'ahu	Gordon S. Chun
39	1954	Moloka'i	Severino
40	Apr. 1955	Hilo, Hawai'i	Kanematsu Oshiro
41	20 Sept. 1955	East Moloka'i	Phillip C. Diez
42*a	13 Dec. 1958	Lanikai, O'ahu	William S. Weaver
43	1950s	Waikīkī, O'ahu	David Lloyd
44	27 Feb. 1960	Mākena, Maui	John Benjamin
45*d	27 Dec. 1960	Maile Point, O'ahu	Harold Riley
46	2 Aug. 1961	Pearl Harbor, O'ahu	Kazuhiko Kato

Swept out to sea while fishing from shore. Victim seen in shark's mouth.

Missing while swimming; shark bite found on right side of body.

Bitten on arm while swimming from fishing boat; shark reported to be in excess of 22 ft.

Bitten on hand while removing shark from net.

Fell off boat while fishing; bitten on leg.

Bitten on thigh while spearfishing close to shore; 10-ft shark observed.

Bitten on leg and foot by 5-ft hammerhead shark while crabbing.

Missing while fishing from shore; body recovered in mutilated condition.

Unprovoked attack, but unable to determine circumstances.

Bitten on hand while fishing from boat.

Bitten on arm while swimming.

Leg amputated while surfing on an air mattress near Mokulua Islands; 15- to 25-ft shark (believed to be tiger shark) observed near body when fire-rescue personnel recovered it 2 hours later. No additional bite marks present on the body.

Provoked attack, but unable to determine circumstances.

Severe lacerations obtained while spearfishing.

Swept out to sea while net fishing; 20-ft shark observed attacking victim; body recovered off Nānākuli.

Bitten on hand by 8-ft shark while net fishing.

Case no.	Date	Location	Victim
47*d	8 Apr. 1963	Hāpuna Beach, Hawai'i	Roy C. Kametani
48	12 Apr. 1963	'Awili, South Kona, Hawai'i	Aiona Aka
49*d	20 Sept. 1967	Kailua Bay, O'ahu	Male
50	9 Mar. 1969	Mākaha, O'ahu	Licius Lee
51	11 Nov. 1969	Barbers Point, O'ahu	D. R. McGinnis
52*c	31 Mar. 1970	Waimea Bay, O'ahu	Ernie Reathaford
53	24 Oct. 1970	Brennecke Beach, Po'ipū, Kaua'i	James C. Mattan
54	16 Mar. 1972	Waihe'e, Wailuku, Maui	Adam Gomes, Jr.
55	17 Aug. 1972	Waimanu, Honoka'a, Hawai'i	Eric Fotherby
56	9 Jan. 1973	Ho'okipa Beach, Pa'ia, Maui	Robert Sterling
57	18 Dec. 1973	Kalama Beach, Kīhei, Maui	Gary W. Floyd
58	10 June 1976	Kama'ole Beach, Park No. 1, Kīhei, Maui	Donald Gard
59*d	16 July 1976	Māhā'ulepū, Kōloa, Kaua'i	Stephen C. Powell

Washed into the sea while picking *'opihi*; parts of body recovered.

Bitten on leg and foot while surfing; 12- to 15-ft shark observed.

Victim lost at sea when boat capsized between O'ahu and Moloka'i; remains of body found in 11-ft tiger shark.

Bitten on leg while surfing; identified as great white shark based on teeth marks in surfboard; dead whale recently removed from the area.

Bitten on tank while scuba diving for lobsters; abrasions on arms and legs and cut on ankle resulting from contact with shark.

Swept out to sea while bodysurfing; 15- to 18-ft shark observed.

Bitten on shoulder and arm while bodysurfing.

Bitten on leg while spearfishing.

Bitten on arm by 8-ft shark while spearfishing.

Bitten on leg while surfboarding close to shore; 4- to 6-ft shark observed in area; wound required 100 stitches.

Bitten on leg while swimming close to shore.

Bitten on foot and leg by 3- to 5-ft shark while swimming.

Missing while scuba diving; lower remains of body recovered.

Case no.	Date	Location	Victim
60*c	1976	Off Lahaina, Maui	Danson Nakaima
61	21 Apr. 1977	Ka'anapali, Maui	Ruskin Vest
62	27 Nov. 1978	'Ewa, O'ahu	Wendell Cabunoc
63*d	1979(?)	South Kohala, Hawai'i	Elderly male
64	4 Aug. 1980	Puamana, Lahaina, Maui	Mark Skidgel
65*d	24 May 1981	Ha'ena Beach Park, Kaua'i	Roger B. Garletts
66*c	12 June 1981	Honoli'i Pali, Hilo Bay('Alae Point), Hawai'i	Preston D. Soley
67*d	24 Aug. 1981	Keaukaha, Hilo, Hawai'i	Ernest Watson
68	9 Nov. 1981	Lā'au Point, Moloka'i	Leo A. Ohai
69	13 Dec. 1981	Nimitz Beach, Barbers Point, O'ahu	Melvin T. Toma
70	14 Feb. 1982	White Plains Beach, Barbers Point, O'ahu	Lisa Miller
71	14 Feb. 1982	White Plains Beach, Barbers Point, O'ahu	Female

Apparently passed out while scuba diving for black coral at a depth of 180 ft. About 30 large sharks seen near partially devoured remains of the body.

Bitten on arm by 4-ft shark while swimming close to shore.

Severely bitten on arm while surfing; 8-ft shark observed.

Disappeared while fishing from shore. Fire Department divers only found a hand and a flashlight.

Bitten on left side of body while resting on a body board 40 ft from shore; identified as 14-ft tiger shark; wound required 52 stitches.

Missing while scuba diving at a depth of 60 to 80 ft; only diving equipment recovered, including shredded wetsuit bearing numerous tooth marks. Victim reportedly spearfishing in murky, choppy water.

Retrieval of floating body hindered by 4-ft shark. Autopsy showed that death was probably from drowning. One-third of body missing due to bites by at least four sharks.

Disappeared while fishing from shore. Leg found 7 days later wedged in rocks 150 yd offshore.

Bitten on hand while untangling crab-trap line from propeller. Seven-foot shark had followed the boat for 3 days and reportedly was very unusual looking with a "flat head."

Severely bitten on right leg by 12-ft tiger shark while swimming at the surface shortly after entering water; site located 300–400 yd from shore over a depth of 20 ft. Looking for fish, but none had been speared when attack occurred; wound required 200 stitches.

Bitten on left leg while wading in 3 to 4 ft of water; 17 stitches required.

Bitten on right foot while swimming in shallow water.

Case no.	Date	Location	Victim
72	13 June 1982	Ho'okipa Beach, Pa'ia, Maui	Scott Shoemaker
73	3 June 1984	Kāne'ohe Bay, O'ahu	Susan Buecher
74	12 Oct. 1985	Barbers Point, O'ahu	Dominic Dela Cruz
75	18 Oct. 1985	Princeville, Kaua'i	Joe Thompson
76*c	20 Apr. 1986	Kalihiwai, Kaua'i	Levi Chandler
77*b	15 Apr. 1987	Kailua-Kona, Hawai'i	Daniel Kennedy
78	25 Mar. 1988	Running Waters Beach, Ninini Point, Kaua'i	Aaron Kawado
79*d	15 Apr. 1988	Waihe'e, Maui	Avery Goo
80*d	8 Jan. 1989	Wailua, Kaua'i	Ken Ahlstrand
81	20 Jan. 1989	Waialua Beach, Moloka'i	Earl Dunnam

Severely bitten three times on the thigh after falling into water while sail boarding 100 yd outside the breakers. Wounds required 120 stitches.

Bitten on the foot while towing her sister on a plastic ski board. Incident happened at 5 P.M. in water 5 ft deep, about 400 yd from shore. Surgery and lower leg cast required to repair damaged tendons; 4- to 5-ft hammerhead shark believed to have been responsible.

Severe gashes to left arm requiring surgery. Attack occurred off Barbers Point Lighthouse while floating on an inner tube after diving for lobster.

Right hand and portion of forearm amputated by a large shark (likely a tiger shark) while body boarding. Gash sustained to left hand. Right anterior side of board also cut away during same bite by shark.

Fell from rocks and disappeared while fishing at Kalihiwai Point. Pieces of clothing and human flesh were recovered by Fire Department divers who encountered a large shark.

Last seen swimming from shore out to an anchored sailboat. Swimming trunks found bitten in half on the bottom.

Bitten on the ankle while bodysurfing in waist-deep water. Surgery required to repair severed vein.

Lost at sea when the 21-ft powerboat he was on capsized in rough seas. Pieces of human stomach, intestines, and pancreas believed to be from victim found several days later washed ashore along the Waihe'e shoreline.

Disappeared while swimming in strong current with three other people. A 2-day search by helicopters, Civil Air Patrol, and firemen failed to find any trace of the missing man. Lower part of body found 6 days later on 14 Jan. 1989 near seawall by the Wailua Golf Course. X-rays of remains revealed teeth marks in femur and tibia.

Ten-year-old boy bitten on the foot by a 6- to 8-ft hammerhead shark. while riding a body board 200 ft from shore. Wound required eight stitches. Bite occurred to a naked foot, and not to the foot wearing a swimfin.

Case no.	Date	Location	Victim
82	3 Apr. 1989	Ho'okipa Beach, Pa'ia, Maui	Sam McLain
83	Apr. 1989	Kekaha Beach, Kaua'i	William P. Allen
84	29 June 1989	Anahola, Kaua'i	Anthony Paden
85*b	14 Oct. 1989	Kahe Point, O'ahu	Ray Mehl, Jr.
86*c	12 Nov. 1989	'Ehukai Beach Park, Sunset Beach, O'ahu	Edward Malek
87	19 Dec. 1989	90 miles east of Hilo, Hawai'i	George Sohswel

Sustained a 4-inch long crescent-shaped wound on the calf while paddling on a surfboard in whitewater near rocks 50 yards from shore. A sharp "tug" was felt at the time of injury; 13 stitches were used to close the wound.

"Tremendous impact" felt on left leg while paddling on a surfboard in glassy water just beyond swells. Impact lifted board and surfer 2–3 ft out of the water. Left thigh raked with a series of scratches believed to have been caused by teeth. Skegs on the board were knocked loose, and a strip of fiberglass 8 inches wide by 5 ft long was torn off. Victim convinced he was attacked by a "huge shark."

Severely bitten on the foot after falling off a surfboard about 20 ft from shore. A "big chunk" taken out of victim's ankle, and "bite marks" inflicted all around the foot. Achilles tendon was half-severed, requiring surgery and a cast.

Abruptly disappeared while scuba diving as a novice with his partner at a depth of 27 ft, 750 ft from shore near the cooling water discharge pipe of the Kahe Point Power Plant. Unusual behavior exhibited by parrotfish just before disappearance. Victim was 10–15 minutes into the dive with nearly a full tank of air. Dive partner conducted a circle search, but could not locate victim. Time of event was 4:30 P.M., visibility 25–30 ft. Decapitated body with amputated left arm found 200 ft to the west by fire rescue divers the following morning. Large tiger shark suddenly appeared and proceeded to consume rest of body before rescue divers could retrieve it. Small piece of flesh and some dive equipment later recovered.

Knocked down and swept away by large waves while wading close to shore at 6 P.M. Lower portion of body, sheared at waistline, recovered by fire rescue personnel on the morning of 15 Nov. 1989, 1.5 miles to the southwest. Note: The rare sighting of a shark was made at 'Ehukai Beach Park on 5 Nov. 1989, at which time all swimmers were cleared from the ocean for an hour.

Crew member of the 51-ft fishing vessel *One Ki* sustained a 23-cm-long bite on his left leg and four 7-cm lacerations to left foot; 3 days hospitalization required. Victim transported to Hilo by Coast Guard helicopter. Wound was inflicted by a shark brought aboard the vessel.

Case no.	Date	Location	Victim
88*b	17 Feb. 1990	Mōkapu, Kāne'ohe Marine Corps Air Station, O'ahu	Roy T. Tanaka
89	1 Apr. 1990	Silver (Silva) Channels, Waialua, O'ahu	Everett Peacock
90	3 Apr. 1991	One'ula Beach Park, 'Ewa Beach, O'ahu	Todd R. Wenke
91	26 May 1991	Mā'ili Beach, O'ahu	Frank (Scott) Betz
92*b	19 Nov. 1991	Māliko Point, Maui	Suk Kyu (Steve) Park

Failed to return with his partner (Jake Hernandez) while scuba diving and spearing parrotfish in water 40 ft deep, 200 yards from shore (near firing range) at 9:30 P.M. 22-ft boat nearby had overturned a short time earlier after being hit broadside by a wave. Victim's tank, backpack, dive light, and mask were found on the bottom but not retrieved. Body with amputated right arm sighted from helicopter at 3 P.M. 18 Feb. 1990 between Makai Pier and Rabbit Island. Two sharks (8 and 14 ft) seen nearby. The larger shark, apparently reacting to the presence of the helicopter, proceeded to consume all but torso and legs before retrieval.

Deep abrasion causing profuse bleeding inflicted to 10-inch area on lower left leg while sitting on a surfboard. Also sustained two deep 3-inch long gashes above left ankle. Event occurred before 7:30 A.M. in murky water 150 yards from shore.

Bitten on the left leg and foot while sitting on a surfboard 350 yards from shore at 5:30 P.M. at a site known as "Shark Country" 1/4 mile east of One'ula Beach Park. Attack resulted in a 5-inch-long bone-deep wound on each side of the foot, and a 9-inch-long bone-deep wound on the calf; 30 stitches, tendon surgery, and a cast required. Only about 18 inches of the shark's head was seen and no positive identification was possible. Shark had "a very large girth."

Bitten on the right calf while sitting on a surfboard 100 yards from shore at 4:45 P.M. Attack resulted in a 4-inch and a 7-inch-long wound requiring stitches. Shark estimated to be 8 ft long. Event occurred in murky water.

Swept into the sea by a large wave while fishing from the rocky coastline at 4:30 P.M. Victim's son went for help shortly thereafter when it became apparent that surf conditions were too rough for his father to swim ashore. When last seen, victim was treading water signaling the son to go for assistance. Help arrived about 30 minutes later, but no sign of the victim could be found. Victim's shorts and shirt were recovered from the ocean bottom the following morning by fire rescue divers. Both garments had large portions missing on the left side. Bite marks present were consistent with attack by a 12-ft tiger shark. Note: Victim was reported to be a strong swimmer in good physical condition.

Case no.	Date	Location	Victim
93*a	26 Nov. 1991	Olowalu, Maui	Martha J. Morrell
94	26 Nov. 1991	Olowalu, Maui	Louise Sourisseau
95*b	19 Feb. 1992	Leftovers, near Waimea Bay, O'ahu	Bryan Adona
96	28 Mar. 1992	Cannons, Hā'ena, Kaua'i	Jude Chamberlain

Snorkeling with a female companion at 9 A.M. near reef edge in partly cloudy water 10–15 ft deep about 100 yards from shore and 50 yards from the end of an old pier next to the victim's beachfront home. An 8- to 11-ft shark passed by the companion and proceeded to attack the victim, initially on the right arm. A small boat was used to recover the body a short time later. Amputations included the victim's right leg at the hip joint, the left leg sheared through the femoral neck, the right forearm, as well as numerous bites and tissue loss elsewhere.

Snorkeling companion to Martha J. Morrell. Abrasion to right calf when large shark rubbed against her in association with fatal attack on Mrs. Morrell. After the initial attack on Mrs. Morrell, the shark, estimated to be 8–11 ft, swam slowly under Louise Sourisseau who assumed a motionless position floating on her back. When first seen before the attack, the shark was coming from a seaward direction. No other significant marine life was observed in the vicinity before or after the attack.

Disappeared while bodyboarding late in the afternoon at a surfing site about 1.2 miles southwest of Waimea Bay (near 61-350 Kamehameha Highway). The following morning, 20 Feb. 1990, his board was found washed ashore at Waimea Bay with a 16-inch crescent-shaped piece missing from the anterior left side. Distinct serrations of shark bite were present in board and severed segment of rubber leash still attached to board. Danny Titilah, the last person to see Bryan Adona alive, saw a large shark shortly after he and Adona paddled out toward separate breaks at Leftovers. Others on shore also reported seeing a large shark in the vicinity. Left swim fin, identified as Bryan Adona's, was subsequently found during an extensive search. Strap of fin was severed, but without serrations.

Scratches and small puncture inflicted to foot when a large shark bit her surfboard while paddling seaward 10 ft from reef edge (and 85 ft from shore) in clean water about 10 ft deep; 12–14 inch crescent bite marks made in both sides of board. Shark shook board three times, then pulled it completely under water and dragged victim by leash for 20 ft before leash severed and shark released surfboard. Attack occurred at about 6:45 A.M. after victim had been surfing there for a short time with a friend (Mike Cox), who witnessed the attack at close range.

Case no.	Date	Location	Victim
97*c	23 July 1992	Wai'anae, O'ahu	Zosimo Popa
98*c	21 Aug. 1992	Twin Arches, Hana Ranch, Maui	Chester N. Shishido
99	22 Oct. 1992	Laniākea, O'ahu	Eric Gruzinsky
100*a	5 Nov. 1992	Kea'au Beach Park, O'ahu	Aaron A. Romento
101	23 Dec. 1992	Chun's Reef, O'ahu	Gary M. Chun

Victim and his son (Jeffrey Popa) failed to return from an overnight fishing trip in a 14-ft boat. Victim's body was found on the morning of 23 July, tied to an ice chest floating 15 miles off the Wai'anae coast. Victim had sustained two cookiecutter shark bites to the lower back. Wounds were 2 inches in diameter by 1.5 inches deep and were "probably post mortem." Cause of death was "asphyxia by drowning." Life jackets and debris were recovered in the vicinity, but victim's son and the boat were never found.

Fell from a cliff while fishing and disappeared in strong current. Rescue efforts were immediately made by victim's brother and, 30 minutes later, at 2:30 P.M., by helicopter and a fire rescue unit. No trace of victim was seen and the search was stopped at 5:30 P.M. Body was recovered the following morning, 22 Aug., 200 yards from shore at a depth of 65 ft. Amputations included the left arm, right hand fractured at the wrist, as well as other numerous lacerations and tissue loss consistent with shark bites that "appeared to be post mortem."

Bruises and scratches to underarm and chest resulting from a 10–12 ft shark biting a crescent-shaped piece from victim's 6 ft 4 in. surfboard. Attack occurred at 7:50 A.M. in clear water 15 ft deep, 150 yards from shore.

Severely bitten in three places on the right leg by a 10–12 ft shark. Victim was bodyboarding at 9:45 A.M. in clear shallow water, 30 yards from shore. Death resulted from blood loss and shock a short time after victim paddled ashore. Wounds did not involve removal of tissue.

Cuts to left hand resulting from 10–12 ft shark biting a 15 in. crescent-shaped piece from victim's surfboard. Attack occurred at 5:30 P.M. while victim was lying on surfboard 100 yards from shore in the presence of 20 or more other surfers. Victim was surfing "near a channel where the current flows like a river through a break in the reef."

Appendix
Checklist of Hawaiian Sharks

For a shark species to appear on this list, the collection of a specimen must have been reliably reported in the scientific literature and/or be on deposit in the collection of a recognized scientist or museum (e.g., Bishop Museum, Honolulu). A few "problematic" species records based on sightings by responsible observers are also included and noted as such in this list. The basis of each such record is explained in the species accounts. References used in assembling this list include Compagno (1984) and Tester (1969).

Species most likely to be encountered by divers and swimmers are marked by an asterisk (*).

In this book a shark is considered to be in "Hawai'i" if it occurs within 200 miles of any island in the full archipelago, from Hawai'i to Kure Atoll.

KEY: Sharks in Hawai'i are usually found in one of three general areas. In the checklist the abbreviations shown in parentheses are used to indicate the general area where one might expect to find a given species:

IN — inshore, relatively shallow waters
OP — offshore pelagic (near the surface, even though water is deep; sometimes shallow-water species are found here, under "fish aggregating devices" [FADs])
D — deep water (i.e., greater than 500 feet)

Alopias pelagicus (pelagic thresher)
Both the English and Hawaiian common names suggest the belief that thresher sharks feed by stunning their prey with strong lashes of their tail. Perhaps they also use the long whiplike fin to herd schooling fish toward their mouths. Thresher sharks caught in the long-line fishery off Hawai'i and in other areas of the central Pacific are often hooked in the tail—not in the mouth like most other fishes caught on long lines. This suggests that the thresher shark was using its tail either to herd the bait or stun it.

117

Order Hexanchiformes
  Family Hexanchidae (sixgill sharks)
    Hexanchias griseus, bluntnose sixgill shark [**D**]
Order Squaliformes (dogfish sharks)
  Family Echinorhinidae (bramble sharks)
    Echinorhinus cookei, prickly shark [**D**]
  Family Squalidae (dogfish sharks)
    Centrophorus tessellatus, mosaic gulper shark [**D**]
    Centroscyllium nigrum, combtooth dogfish [**D**]
    Dalatias licha, kitefin shark [**D**]
    Etmopterus villosus, Hawaiian lanternshark [**D**]
    Euprotomicrus bispinatus, pygmy shark [**D**]
    Isistius brasiliensis, cookiecutter shark [**D, OP**]
    Squalus asper, roughskin spurdog [**D**]
    Squalus mitsukurii, shortspine spurdog [**D**]
Order Orectolobiformes (carpet sharks)
  Family Rhincodontidae
    Rhincodon typus *, whale shark [**IN, OP**]
Order Lamniformes (mackerel sharks)
  Family Odontaspididae
    Odontaspis ferox, smalltooth sand tiger [**OP**]
  Family Pseudocarchariidae (crocodile sharks)
    Pseudocarcharias kamoharai, crocodile shark [**OP**]
  Family Megachasmidae
    Megachasma pelagios, megamouth shark [**D, OP**]
  Family Alopiidae (thresher sharks)
    Alopias pelagicus, pelagic thresher shark [**OP**]
    Alopias superciliosus, bigeye thresher [**OP**]

PHOTO BY HOWARD HALL

Alopias vulpinus, thresher shark [**OP**]
Family Cetorhinidae (basking sharks)
   Cetorhinus maximus, basking shark [**OP**]
Family Lamnidae (mackerel sharks, etc.)
   Carcharodon carcharias, great white shark* [**IN**]
   Isurus oxyrinchus, shortfin mako* [**IN**]
   Isurus paucus, longfin mako* [**OP**]
Order Carcharhiniformes (ground sharks)
   Family Pseudotriakidae (false cat sharks)
      Pseudotriakis microdon, false cat shark [**D**]
   Family Triakidae
      Galeorhinus galeus, tope shark [**IN**]
   Family Carcharhinidae (requiem sharks)
      Carcharinus altimus, bignose shark* [**OP**]
      C. amblyrhynchos, gray reef shark* [**IN**]
      C. falciformis, silky shark* [**OP**]
      C. galapagensis, galapagos shark* [**IN**]
      C. limbatus, blacktip shark* [**IN**]
      C. longimanus, oceanic whitetip shark*
      C. melanopterus, blacktip reef shark* [**IN**]
      C. plumbeus, sandbar shark* [**IN**]
      Galeocerdo cuvier, tiger shark* [**IN**]
      Prionace glauca, blue shark [**OP**]
      Triaenodon obesus, whitetip reef shark* [**IN**]
   Family Sphyrnidae (hammerhead sharks)
      Sphyrna lewini, scalloped hammerhead* [**IN**]
      S. zygaena, smooth hammerhead* [**IN**]

GLOSSARY OF HAWAIIAN TERMS

'ahi   large tuna; refers to both *Thunnus obesus* (bigeye tuna) and *Thunnus albacares* (yellowfin tuna).

ali'i   royal or noble person or royal group, e.g., chief, chiefess, king, queen.

'aumakua   family or personal god taking the form of a living organism of the land or sea.

'awa   diluted juice of the roots of the **kava** plant (*Piper methysticum*) noted throughout the Pacific Islands for its mild druglike effects.

heiau   sacred sites dedicated to worship; usually stone or earth platforms with simple to elaborate structures.

ho'omanō   to behave like a shark; to eat ravenously; to pursue women ardently.

humuhumunukunukuāpua'a
either of two common triggerfish occurring on Hawaiian reefs, *Rhinecanthus rectangulus*, or *R. aculeatus*. Noted by modern residents as the state fish of Hawaii.

kahu manō   an attendant or guardian of an individual shark that is believed to be filled with a special spirit.

kahuna   a priest or highly respected expert.

kapa   fabric made by treating and pounding the bark of certain trees and shrubs, e.g. **wauke** (*Broussonetia papyrifera*).

kapu   forbidden or prohibited; sometimes used selectively, for certain seasons or certain groups.

kīholo   large, mainly wooden, fishhook used for sharks and large fish.

koa   large native forest tree, and the useful, valuable wood from it (*Acacia koa*).

koa'e'ula   red-tailed tropic bird (*Phaethon rubricauda*), a seabird noted for its slender, elongated tailfeathers.

Kohala   the land district on the western and northwestern area of the island of Hawai'i.

kupua   a demi-god or supernatural being, possessing several forms, usually human and animal.

lālākea   reef shark with white fins; probably refers to the whitetip reef shark, (*Triaenodon obesus*).

lālani kalalea
    line of shark fins protruding above the surface of the water.

laukāhi'u   probably refers to thresher sharks (*Alopias* spp.); literally means "much hit tail."

leiomano   a weapon or tool crafted from wood and shark teeth.

lele wa'a   according to Mary Pukui (in the *Hawaiian Dictionary*), "the friendly shark said to lean on canoe outriggers for food and company." May refer to the whale shark (*Rhincodon typus*); see pages 30–31 for discussion.

mana   supernatural or divine power and authority.

manō   general name for shark, often modified with descriptive adjectives; refers to species other than very large dangerous sharks (*see* **niuhi**).

manō kanaka
    a shark thought to be born of a human mother and sired by a shark god, or by a deified person whose spirit possesses a shark or turns into a shark.

manō kihikihi
    hammerhead shark (*Sphyrna* spp.); literally translates as "angular shark."

manō pā'ele   literally translates as "black-smudged shark"; perhaps refers to the blacktip reef shark (*Carcharhinus melanopterus*) or the blacktip shark (*C. limbatus*).

manō 'ula   literally translates as "red shark"; see page 29 for discussion.

melomelo   wooden club or stick, soaked or rubbed with bait and used as an attractant for fish.

niuhi   defined by the *Hawaiian Dictionary* as "a large gray man-eating shark." This is probably a general term (like **manō**) and refers to the great white shark (*Carcharodon carcharias*), the tiger shark (*Galeocerdo cuvier*), and perhaps other species of large, dangerous sharks.

pāhoehoe   basaltic lava characterized, in part, by a smooth surface.

paniolo   cowboy; horseman noted for skill in handling cattle.

pau   finished, completed, done with.

tapa   *See* **kapa**.

'ula   red, scarlet; also short for **koa'e 'ula**, the red-tailed tropic bird.

'unihipili   spirit of a dead person present in the remains (e.g., bones or hair), which can be transferred into the living form of a creature such as a shark.

wa'a   canoe, especially a large, double-hulled canoe.

BIBLIOGRAPHY

Anonymous,1976. Pu'ukoholā Heiau: National Historic Site, Hawaii. Washington, D.C.: National Park Service, U.S. Department of Commerce GDP 1976-211–313/103: 1–4.

Balazs, G. H., 1987. Annotated list of shark attacks in the Hawaiian Islands. *Hawaii Fishing News* 12(8): 12–13.

———, 1992. Annotated list of shark attacks in the Hawaiian Islands. *Hawaii Fishing News* 16(12): 6–8.

Balazs, G. H., and A. K. H. Kam, 1981. A review of shark attacks in the Hawaiian Islands. *'Elepaio* 41(10): 97–106.

———, 1983. A history of shark attacks in Hawaii. *Honolulu Magazine* 17(10): 58–63, 94.

Beckwith, M., 1970. *Hawaiian Mythology.* Honolulu: University of Hawaii Press. Reprint of 1940 Yale University Press edition.

Buck, P. H., 1964. Arts and Crafts of Hawaii VII: Fishing. *Bishop Museum Special Publication.* 45: 285–585.

Castro, J. I., 1983. *The Sharks of North American Waters.* College Station, Texas: Texas A&M University Press.

Clark, E., 1981. Sharks: Magnificent and Misunderstood. *National Geographic* 160: 138–187

Clarke, T. A., 1971. The Ecology of the Scalloped Hammerhead Shark, *Sphyrna lewini,* in Hawaii. *Pacific Science* 25: 133–144.

Compagno, L. J. V., 1984. *Sharks of the World.* Rome: United Nations Food and Agriculture Organization Fisheries Synopsis 125, vol. 4, parts 1 and 2.

———, 1988. *Sharks of the Order Carcharhiniformes.* Princeton, New Jersey: Princeton University Press.

Cook, S., 1985. *Sharks: An Inquiry into Biology, Behavior, Fisheries, and Use.* Portland, Oregon: Oregon State University Extension Service.

Crow, G. L., and J. D. Hewitt IV, 1988. Longevity Records for Captive Tiger Sharks. *International Zoo Yearbook* 27: 237–240.

De Crosta, M. A., 1984. Age Determination, Growth, and Energetics of Three Species of Carcharhinid Sharks in Hawaii. University of Hawaii, Masters thesis.

Ellis, R., 1976. *The Book of Sharks.* New York: Grosset and Dunlap.

———, 1983. *The Book of Sharks.* New York: Harcourt Brace Jovanovich, revised edition.

Ellis, R., and J. E. McCosker, 1991. *Great White Shark.* New York: HarperCollins.

Emerson, J. S., 1892. The Lesser Hawaiian Gods. *Hawaiian Historical Society Papers* (no. 2): 1–24.

Feher, J., 1969. *Hawaii: A Pictorial History*. Honolulu: Bishop Museum Press.

Ferguson, A., and G. Cailliet, 1990. *Sharks and Rays of the Pacific Coast*. Monterey, California: Monterey Bay Aquarium Foundation.

Garrick, J. A. F., 1982. Sharks of the Genus *Carcharhinus*. NOAA Tech. Report 445. Washington, D.C.: U.S. Department of Commerce.

Gruber, S. H., ed., 1991. *Discovering Sharks. A volume honoring the work of Stewart Springer*. Highlands, New Jersey: American Littoral Society.

Handy, E. S. C., and M. K. Pukui, 1972. *The Polynesian Family System in Ka'u, Hawai'i*. Rutland, Vermont: Charles E. Tuttle.

Holland, K., B. M. Wetherbee, J. D. Peterson, and C. G. Lowe, 1993. Movements and Distribution of Hammerhead Shark Pups on Their Natal Grounds. *Copeia* 3 (in press).

Johnson, R. H., 1978. *Sharks of Polynesia*. Les Editions du Pacifique.

Jones, E.C., 1971. *Isistius brasiliensis*, a Squaloid Shark, the Probable Cause of Crater Wounds on Fishes and Cetaceans. *Fish. Bull. NOAA/NMFS* 69: 791–798.

Kamakau, S. M., 1976. *The Works of the People of Old*. Honolulu: Bishop Museum Press.

Kato, S., S. Springer, and M. H. Wagner, 1967. *Field Guide to Eastern Pacific and Hawaiian Sharks*. Washington, D.C.: U.S. Department of the Interior.

Klimley, A. P., 1981. Grouping Behavior in the Scalloped Hammerhead. *Oceanus* 24 (4): 65–71.

Lavenberg, R. J., 1991. Megamania. The Continuing Saga of Megamouth Sharks. *Terra* 30 (1): 28–39.

Lineaweaver, T. H. I., and R. H. Backus, 1970. *The Natural History of Sharks*. Philadelphia and New York: J.B. Lippincott Company.

McMahon, Bucky, 1993. "Lord Long Arms, I Presume?" *Outside* 18: 62–67, 131–135.

Michael, Scott W., 1993. *Reef Sharks and Rays of the World. A Guide to Their Identification, Behavior, and Ecology*. Monterey, California: Sea Challengers.

Pukui, M. K., 1983. *'Ōlelo No'eau: Hawaiian Proverbs and Poetical Sayings*. Bishop Museum Special Publication 71.

Pukui, M. K., and S. H. Elbert, 1971. *Hawaiian Dictionary*. Honolulu: University of Hawaii Press.

Pukui, M. K., S. H. Elbert, and R. Johnson, 1971. Glossary of Hawaiian Gods, Demigods, Family Gods, and a Few Heroes. Supplement B. *Hawaiian Dictionary*. Honolulu: University of Hawaii Press.

Pukui, M. K., S. H. Elbert, and E.T. Mookini, 1974. *Place Names of Hawaii*. Honolulu: University of Hawaii Press.

Pukui, M. K., E. W. Haertig, and C. A. Lee, 1972. *Nānā I Ke Kumu [Look to the Source]*. Honolulu: Hui Hanai, Queen Lili'uokalani Children's Center.

Randall, J. E., 1977. Contribution to the Biology of the Whitetip Reef Shark. *Pacific Science* 31 (2): 143–164.

Randall, J. E., and G. S. Helfman, 1973. Attacks on Humans by the Blacktip Reef Shark *Carcharhinus melanopterus. Pacific Science* 27 (3): 226–238.

Scott, E., 1968. *Saga of the Sandwich Islands.* Lake Tahoe: Sierra-Tahoe Publishers.

Strasberg, D. W., 1958. Distribution, Abundance, and Habits of Pelagic Sharks in the Central Pacific Ocean. *Fish. Bull. U.S. Fish and Wildlife Service* 58: 335–361.

Taylor, L., 1977a. Megamouth. *Oceans* 10: 46–47.

———, 1977b. How to Avoid Shark Attack—If You Happen to Be a Hawaiian Monk Seal. *Oceans Magazine* 10 (6): 21–23.

———, 1985. "White Sharks in Hawaii: Historical and Contemporary Records." In Sibley, G., editor. *Biology of the White Shark.* Fullerton, California: Southern California Academy of Sciences: 41–48.

———, 1988. Shark Attack in the Tropical Pacific Ocean. In *Sharks,* J. D. Stevens, editor. Hong Kong: Intercontinental Publishing.

Taylor, L., and R. S. Nolan, 1978. Mini, the Friendly Whale Shark. *Sea Frontiers* 24 (3): 169–176.

Taylor, L., and M. Wisner, 1989. Growth Rates of Captive Blacktip Reef Sharks, *Carcharhinus melanopterus. Bulletin de l'Inst. Oceanog., Monaco* Special Number 5: 211–217.

Tester, A. L., 1969. *Cooperative Shark Research and Control Program: Final Report 1968–69.* Department of Zoology, University of Hawaii.

Tricas, T. C., and L. Taylor, 1981. Diel Behavior of the Tiger Sharks, *Galeocerdo cuvier,* at French Frigate Shoals, Hawaiian Islands. *Copeia* 1981 (4): 904–908.

Volpe, E. P., 1976. *Recent Advances in the Biology of Sharks.* New Orleans: American Society of Zoologists.

von Tempski, A., 1940. *Born in Paradise.* Woodbridge, Connecticut: Ox Bow Press.

Wass, R. C., 1971. A Comparative Study of the Life History, Distribution and Ecology of the Sandbar Shark and the Gray Reef Shark. Ph.D. thesis, Zoology Department, University of Hawaii.

———, 1973. Size, Growth and Reproduction of the Sandbar Shark, *Carcharhinus milberti,* in Hawaii. *Pacific Science* 27 (4): 305–318.

TAXONOMIC INDEX

(illustrations in **boldface**)

shortfin mako **46**, 47, **66**, 66, 80, **81**
shortspine spurdog **55**, 55
silky shark **71**, 71
silvertip shark **69**, 69
smalltooth sand tiger **58**, 58
smooth hammerhead **80**, 80
Sphyrna lewini **78**, 78, **82**, 83
Sphyrna zygaena 78, **80**, 80
Sphyrnidae 119
Squalidae 118
Squaliformes 118
Squalus asper **55**, 55
Squalus mitsukurii **55**, 55

thresher shark **63**, 63, 85
tiger shark **cover**, iv, **10**, **13**, 25, **28**, **29**, 31, 32, 33, **36**, 38, 39, 40, **41**, **43**, 66, **76**, 76, **84**, 85, 89, 90, 91, 99, 103, 107, 109, 113, 117
tope shark **68**, 68
Triaenodon obesus 30, 74, **77**, 77, 78
Triakidae 119

whale shark 3, **13**, **17**, **30**, **31**, **49**, **56**, **57**, 61, 64
whitetip reef shark 3, **14**, **20**, **21**, 74, **77**, 77, 78, 83, **86**, 86

INDEX OF SELECTED HAWAIIAN TERMS